Future Publishing Ltd, Unit 415 Eskdale Road, Winnersh Triangle Business Park, Winnersh, Reading, RG41 5TU
0330 390 6591; www.countrylife.co.uk

Long to reign over us

Everywhere in the world, whenever anyone refers to 'The Queen', they mean only 'Our Queen'. In this special issue, we salute the remarkable Elizabeth II

TODAY, for the majority of us, the world seems an almost unrecognisable place. Most of us haven't experienced a Great Britain or a Commonwealth that isn't under the unwavering leadership of Elizabeth II. It feels as if the nation has lost a crucial family member—its beloved, respected grandmother—and mourns accordingly.

That The Queen seemed serenely unchangeable over her long reign is all the more remarkable when one considers the events that occurred during her lifetime. She was born into a world still shaken after the First World War and that, within weeks of her birth, was then plunged into extreme poverty following the Wall Street Crash. Although she was born into a household of wealth and privilege, her parents instilled in her a strong sense of frugality and the importance of leading the nation by example, traits from which she never wavered and has passed on through the generations.

Although her early childhood was idyllic, the family was sorely tested by the abdication of her uncle, Edward VIII, followed by another devastating global conflict. Princess Elizabeth was able to rejoice anonymously amid the throngs filling the Mall on VE Day and her wedding was a ray of hope in the post-Second World War gloom. Such was the people's affection for her that they tried to help provide her wedding dress by donating their own clothing ration coupons. Sadly, it wasn't long after this happy day when her father's precarious health failed and she took the throne.

Her own long reign has seen many changes and upheavals throughout society, which she matched with changes in how the Royal Family and Buckingham Palace work. It's hard to believe that the now-familiar royal walkabouts are a comparatively recent phenomenon, but they brought The Queen much closer to her people, who responded with overwhelming affection.

National and international leaders came and went, but The Queen remained and her long years of experience made her a respected statesman, her advice and opinion carrying the weight of years,

'The baton will go on and we won't let you down'

all delivered with a gentle hand. In an era when it seems everyone wishes to be famous for nothing, The Queen never sought to court popular opinion by appealing to the lowest common denominator.

Paying tribute to her on the eve of her Diamond Jubilee in 2012, her grandson The Duke of Cambridge emphasised her lack of interest in celebrity: 'That's not what monarchy's about. It's about setting examples. It's about doing one's duty, as she would say. It's about using your position for the good. It's about serving the country.' These were things she did without hesitation or limit.

The Commonwealth and its success were particularly dear to her heart, knowing as she did how important it is for the nations to come together, but without wishing to bind them. In 2011, President Mohamed Nasheed of the Maldives declared how the organisation regarded Her Majesty: 'In our minds, she's not necessarily just English. She doesn't have a nationality... She's the first [British] monarch to have engaged the world, not as an Imperial ruler, but someone who is out there to look after us in a sense.'

She guided her own family in the same manner, allowing them to find their own style and make their own mistakes, but being an invaluable source of support and knowledge.

Speaking in 2011, Prince William summed up his grandmother's reign. 'She's so dedicated and really determined to finish everything she started. She'll want to hand over knowing she's done everything she possibly could to help and that she's got no regrets and no unfinished business; that she's done everything she can for the country and that she's not let anyone down—she minds an awful lot about that.' No one can doubt that she has succeeded in those aims and exceeded them day in, day out for decades.

It's an example we should all try to follow. As Baroness Scotland, Secretary-General of the Commonwealth, has put it: 'The baton will go on and we won't let you down.'

For now, we are sure you will join us in saying thank you, ma'am —we'll miss you.

Editor Mark Hedges

Project Editor/Chief Sub-Editor Jane Watkins

Deputy Chief Sub-Editor Octavia Pollock

Head of Design Dean Usher

Design Heather Clark, Sarah Readman, Ben Harris

Picture Editor Lucy Ford

Deputy Picture Editor Emily Anderson

Picture research Sue Nicholls

(ipso.) Regulated

Happy & glorious

The words of the National Anthem are an apt, if inadequate, description of Elizabeth II's life and reign and the affection in which she was held by her subjects

I T only took four words to change the nation completely: 'London Bridge is down.' These words, delivered immediately upon The Queen's death, put into motion a series of steps long decided upon and revised many times over the monarch's record-breaking reign since the plan was first drawn up in the 1960s.

The first person told was The Prince of Wales and then, before long, the news spread to the Prime Minister, overseas governments, the media and, finally, a population that was plunged into grief for the only ruler that most of its members had ever known. The ripples soon spread to the wider world, which joined in the shock at the end of an era.

Plans decades in the making swung into motion. Television stations had long prepared six days of tributes and reactions —using the codename Mrs Robinson—and who will forget the dignity of the new King as he spoke to the nation and the Commonwealth before announcing plans to visit the country, treating his grieving subjects with kindness and thoughtfulness? Long lines snaked across the country as millions filed

to sign books of condolence and many millions more paid tribute in their own way —although it has been a time of great solemnity, most of us will have brought to mind happy images of The Queen throughout her reign.

'Throughout all my life and with all my heart, I shall strive to be worthy of your trust'

Elizabeth II

This publication is a celebration of the tireless work Elizabeth II undertook on our behalf, of the love she had for her people and the love they had—and have—for her and of that indefinable something that makes the pomp and ceremony of Britain so attractive. It will contain both the magnificent state occasions and the more intimate moments, as well as the times of joy and of sadness that have filled the years

of someone who became the most famous and photographed person in the world during a life that spanned almost a century.

And what a life it was! Comparing the world that Elizabeth was born into in 1926 with the one she has left is apt to leave one breathless at the pace of change—in 1926, there were few cars and phones and no television or computers.

It was a lifespan that saw momentous events, from the Second World War to a man on the Moon. Equally as amazing have been the changes in society and The Queen not only weathered these, but embraced them enthusiastically.

Yes, she will be missed, but she will not be forgotten—the Second Elizabethan Age has been far too remarkable for that. She can rest serenely in the knowledge that the succession is secure for several generations to come. So, for probably the last time, let us all declare: 'God save our gracious Queen!' ➤

Above: Princess Elizabeth with her doting parents, the Duke and Duchess of York. *Facing page:* A happy life on the ocean wave: carefree aboard *Britannia* in 1971

The Queen and Prince Philip extend a warm welcome to the newborn Archie Mountbatten-Windsor, son of The Duke and Duchess of Sussex, in 2019, together with Meghan's mother, Doria Ragland ➤

Above: Enjoying the Braemar Highland Games with The Prince of Wales in 2012. *Above left:* The Second World War brought some freedom for mechanic Second Subaltern Windsor. *Above right:* The success of the Commonwealth has been of abiding importance for The Queen

A visibly amused Queen and Prince Philip give a swarm of bees a wide berth at a review of the Grenadier Guards at Windsor Castle in 2003

Smile please, Ma'am: the world's most photographed woman gives one lucky member of the crowd the perfect picture ✎

Long to reign over us

1926 At 2.40am on April 21, the first child of the Duke and Duchess of York, Elizabeth Alexandra Mary, was born by caesarean section at her maternal grandfather's London home—17, Bruton Street in Mayfair

1936 After the abdication of her uncle, Edward VIII, her father succeeded to the throne and she became heir presumptive

1940 Princess Elizabeth made her first public speech at the age of 14, to all the children of Britain and the Commonwealth

1945 The Princess joined the war effort and trained as a driver in the Women's Auxiliary Territorial Service

1947 She married Lt Philip Mountbatten in Westminster Abbey on November 20

1948 Prince Charles born on November 14

1950 Princess Anne born on August 15

1952 Elizabeth became Queen on February 6, following the death of her father

1953 After a year of planning, the Coronation took place in Westminster Abbey on June 2

1960 Prince Andrew born on February 19

1964 Prince Edward born on March 10

1965 The Queen broadcast her first Commonwealth Day message, addressing issues facing the organisation

1977 The Silver Jubilee was celebrated, with street parties across the country

1977 The birth of her first grandchild, Peter Phillips. He was followed by Zara Phillips (1981), Prince William (1982), Prince Harry (1984), Princess Beatrice (1988), Princess Eugenie (1990), Lady Louise Windsor (2003) and Viscount Severn (2007)

1993 The Queen allowed the State Rooms of Buckingham Palace to be opened for the first time to the public during the summer, a practice that has continued every year since, with special exhibitions a particular draw

The Queen had an eventful life—here are some of the most memorable events in her personal timeline

2002 A shadow was cast over the Golden Jubilee by the deaths of The Queen's sister, Princess Margaret (February 9), and Queen Elizabeth, the Queen Mother (March 30)

2009 The Duke of Edinburgh became Britain's longest-serving consort

2010 The birth of The Queen's first great-grand-child, Savannah Phillips. She was followed by Isla Phillips (2012), Prince George (2013), Mia Tindall (2014), Princess Charlotte (2015), Prince Louis and Lena Phillips (2018), Archie Mountbatten-Windsor (2019), August Brooksbank, Lucas Tindall, Lilibet Mountbatten-Windsor and Sienna Mapelli Mozzi (2021)

2011 Prince William, second-in-line to the throne, married Catherine Middleton on April 29 at Westminster Abbey, watched by a UK audience of 36.7 million

2012 The Diamond Jubilee came in what proved to be a resoundingly positive year for the UK, followed as it was by the London Olympics. It meant that Her Majesty was the first head of state to open two Olympic Games in two different countries—not to mention to appear as a Bond Girl

2015 She became the longest-reigning British monarch, as well as the longest-reigning queen regnant and female head of state in the world on September 9

2016 The Queen became the world's longest currently reigning monarch on October 13, following the death of Rama IX of Thailand, and the oldest current head of state

2017 On her 70th wedding anniversary, The Queen said: 'I don't know that anyone had invented the term "platinum" for a 70th wedding anniversary. When I was born, you weren't expected to be around that long'

2019 On January 31, The Queen became the longest-reigning female ruler ever, over-taking Eleanor (1122–1204), who was Queen Consort of France and England and Duchess of Aquitaine for 66 years and 358 days

2021 The Duke of Edinburgh dies, aged 99

Country Life Commemorative Issue

17

Party time: The Queen and The Duke of Edinburgh prepare to meet the crowds at a Buckingham Palace garden party in 2014.
Royal commentator Robert Hardman estimated that Her Majesty had met the equivalent of the population of New Zealand since ascending the throne

Measuring the ruler

How many miles did The Queen travel? Who has to give her pasties?
Of what could she do an uncanny impression?

Written by Jane Watkins

Display by the New Covent Garden Flower Market at the Chelsea Flower Show in 2016

I T'S been a remarkable reign however you look at it and Her Majesty became so woven into the fabric of our lives that we simply took her existence for granted. We seldom stopped to think about such things as the sheer number of people she met each day, let alone each year, and how that already staggering figure accumulated decade upon decade and continued well past the point at which most of us would have wanted to put work aside.

In her later years, royal commentators began to tally up the people met, the miles travelled, the honours bestowed, the records broken and the incomparable set of 'firsts', from visits to China and Russia to technological changes, such as websites and emails, and societal changes. The results seem impossible for one person to have achieved, especially for someone who had huge responsibility thrust on her at such a young age.

In 1952, she declared: 'My Father, and my Grandfather before him, worked hard all their lives to unite our peoples ever more closely, and to maintain its ideals which were so near to their hearts. I shall strive to carry on their work.' Not once did she fail them, but carried out that work in ways of which they could never have conceived.

Over the next few pages, we shine a spotlight on some of the facts and figures that have underpinned the many decades The Queen devoted to us ungrudgingly. The Second Elizabethan Age will surely go down in history as a truly golden period.

Putting the royal in mail

So unchanging were the essential elements of The Queen's appearance that our stamps continued to feature an image created by the sculptor Arnold Machin in 1966, taken from a portrait photograph by Prof John Hedgecoe

▬▬▬

Because Britain invented the stamp, our stamps don't need to have 'United Kingdom' printed on them, but the monarch's head always appears

▬▬▬

The Queen approved all new designs, including commemorative and special ones

A special design of the 1st class stamp was produced in 2012. The traditional gold was replaced with a blue colour scheme and the words 'Diamond Jubilee' highlighted in iridescent ink

▬▬▬

The Queen inherited George V's stamp collection, which was housed in 328 red albums of about 60 pages. It was added to after his death—those collected by George VI are kept in blue albums and boxes and those by Elizabeth II in green albums and boxes. John Tilleard was the first Philatelist to the King and the last Keeper (as the curator is known) was Michael Sefi

Keeping in touch

3.5 million items of correspondence were received and answered

▬▬▬

More than 175,000 telegrams were sent to centenarians, although only one, that to the Queen Mother, was signed Lilibet

▬▬▬

The Queen sent more than 540,000 telegrams to couples celebrating their diamond wedding anniversary

▬▬▬

When she married Prince Philip, the couple received more than 2,500 wedding presents from all over the world, as well as some 10,000 telegrams of congratulation

Some 20,000 cards were received on The Queen's 80th birthday

▬▬▬

130,000 messages of congratulation and goodwill were received in the Diamond Jubilee

▬▬▬

The Queen and the Duke of Edinburgh sent more than 45,000 Christmas cards and gave more than 90,000 Christmas puddings to their staff. Every year, The Queen sent Christmas trees to Westminster Abbey, Wellington Barracks, St Paul's Cathedral, St Giles and The Canongate Kirk in Edinburgh, Crathie Church near Balmoral and local Sandringham schools and churches

Going online and beyond

1969 A message of the Queen's congratulations to Apollo 11 astronauts for the first Moon landing was microfilmed and left on the satellite's surface

▬▬▬

1976 The Queen became the first monarch to send an email. Her username was HME2

▬▬▬

1997 The official website www.royal.gov.uk was set up

▬▬▬

2007 The official British Monarchy YouTube channel was opened

▬▬▬

2009 The Royal Twitter account was launched (@RoyalFamily)

▬▬▬

2010 Facebook (www.facebook.com/TheBritishMonarchy), Instagram (www.instagram.com/theroyalfamily) and Flickr (www.flickr.com/photos/britishmonarchy) pages were added

▬▬▬

2014 The Queen sent her first tweet under her own name at the Science Museum: 'It is a pleasure to open the Information Age exhibition today at the @ScienceMuseum and I hope people will enjoy visiting. Elizabeth R'

Queen of the world

▸ The *Daily Telegraph* estimated that The Queen travelled 1,032,513 miles on state or Commonwealth tours during her reign—or the equivalent of 42 journeys around the circumference of the globe. The actual total will be much higher as the figure assumes mileage 'as the crow flies' and doesn't include any travel when in the different countries. For example, on her first Australia tour, she averaged 230 miles a day, making 35 internal flights and travelling 13,000 miles

▸ In the six-month Commonwealth Tour of 1953–54, her first as Queen, 43,618 miles were travelled. She visited Bermuda, Jamaica, Panama, Fiji, Tonga, New Zealand, Australia, the Cocos Islands, Ceylon, Aden, Uganda, Libya, Malta and

Above: The Queen was seen to wipe away a tear when *Britannia* was decommissioned.
Below: In 1994, she became the only British monarch ever to visit Russia

Gibraltar. At one Australian function, she was given 161 bouquets; at another, five tons of dried fruit

▸ She travelled to more countries than any previous British monarch: 120 in all

▸ She made 82 state visits and received more than 150 inward state visits

▸ Official visits have ranged from the tiny Cocos Islands, at some five square miles, with a population of 596, to vast China, at 3.7 million square miles, with a population of 1.41 billion

▸ In 1974, The Queen had to bring a visit to Australia and Indonesia to an abrupt end when a snap general election was called. It was the first time a sovereign had had to interrupt an overseas tour

▸ She learnt to drive in 1945, but she didn't have a driving licence and wasn't obliged to show numberplates. As all UK passports were issued in her name, she didn't need one

▸ To celebrate her Silver Jubilee, The Queen carried out six tours in three months that took her through 36 counties in the UK. It's estimated that she and the Duke of Edinburgh travelled 56,000 miles that year

▸ The Royal Yacht *Britannia* travelled more than one million miles in the more than 43 years (1954–97) that she was in use, an average of 25,000 miles a year. Prince Charles and Princess Anne sailed on her before The Queen did

During The Queen's reign, there have been...

Fifteen Prime Ministers
Winston Churchill, Anthony Eden, Harold Macmillan, Alec Douglas-Holme, Harold Wilson, Ted Heath, James Callaghan, Margaret Thatcher, John Major, Tony Blair, Gordon Brown, David Cameron, Theresa May, Boris Johnson and Liz Truss

Fourteen Presidents
Harry S. Truman, Dwight D. Eisenhower, John F. Kennedy, Lyndon B. Johnson, Richard Nixon, Gerald Ford, Jimmy Carter, Ronald Reagan, George H. W. Bush, Bill Clinton, George W. Bush, Barack Obama, Donald Trump and Joe Biden

Seven Archbishops of Canterbury
Geoffrey Fisher, Michael Ramsey, Donald Coggan, Robert Runcie, George Carey, Rowan Williams and Justin Welby

Seven Popes
Pius XII, John XXIII, Paul VI, John Paul I, John Paul II, Benedict XVI and Francis I

'There is no one whose counsel I would wish to seek... more than The Queen's'

Sir John Major

'Winston, of course, because it was always such fun'

Elizabeth II's reply when she was asked who had been her favourite Prime Minister

Top left: The height of embarrassment: George Bush's team fails to adjust the microphones on a 1991 trip to the White House

Top right: The Queen on a state visit to Pope John Paul II at the Vatican in 1980. She met five Popes, most recently Francis I

Coronation

27 million
people in the UK watched it on television
(about half of the population).
For some, it was the first thing they had
ever seen on the small screen

—

3 million
thronged the pavements along the route

—

8,251
members of the congregation inside
Westminster Abbey

—

29,200
British, colonial and Commonwealth
troops lined the route

A record-breaking reign

Four out of five people living in Britain now weren't even born when Elizabeth II came to the throne

***

She was only the second British monarch to achieve a Golden Jubilee or 60-year reign and the first to achieve a Sapphire Jubilee (65 years)

***

The Queen was the 40th monarch since William the Conqueror and the 39th to be crowned at Westminster Abbey

***

She became the longest-serving queen regnant and head of state on September 9, 2015

On January 31, 2019, she became the longest-reigning female ruler ever, beating the record set by Eleanor of Aquitaine (1122–1204), who ruled for 66 years and 358 days as Queen Consort of France and England and Duchess of Aquitaine

***

Elizabeth II became the longest-reigning living monarch on October 13, 2016, on the death of Rama IX of Thailand and the oldest current head of state on November 21, 2017, following Robert Mugabe's resignation

The Queen had the longest marriage of any British monarch and was the only one to celebrate a platinum wedding anniversary

***

Prince Charles was the longest-serving heir apparent both in Britain and the world and the longest-serving Prince of Wales

***

Elizabeth II was the first member of the Royal Family to receive a gold disc: the CD *Party at the Palace* sold 100,000 copies in its first week of release in 2002 (the performance included Brian May, *above*)

Let's get personal

She was named Elizabeth after her mother, Alexandra after George V's mother, who had died six months previously, and Mary after her paternal grandmother. She was called Lilibet by her close family, based on what she called herself as a child

Her full title was Elizabeth II, by the Grace of God of the United Kingdom of Great Britain and Northern Ireland and of Her other Realms and Territories Queen, Head of the Commonwealth, Defender of the Faith

In the Channel Islands, she was known as The Duke of Normandy and, in the Isle of Man, Lord of Mann. She was also The Duke of Lancaster

***

She was about 5ft 3in tall

What's in a name: things named after Elizabeth II

- 40 buildings, including the Elizabeth Tower (*above*), home of Big Ben
- 3 awards for service and gallantry
- 8 awards for leadership and innovation
- 5 awards for the Arts
- 53 geographical locations (including lakes, mines, towns, parks and so on)
- 9 races and competitions
- 28 hospitals and health centres
- 34 roadways
- 7 bridges
- 3 trains

- 14 monuments, including two statues in which she's carrying a handbag, at Spring Hill, Brisbane, and at Government House, Adelaide, both in Australia
- 34 schools and colleges
- 1 capsule on the London Eye
- 1 London Underground line and 1 train line
- 1 bell (at St James Garlickhythe in the City)
- 1 cake
- 1 Queen Elizabeth rose, but it has several colour sports, in white, coral, yellow and apricot. There

is also the sport Climbing Queen Elizabeth and a hybrid called Scarlet Queen Elizabeth

- In the 1960s, scientist Sir Peter Scott offered to name the Loch Ness Monster *Elizabethia nessiae* in a bid to boost its profile. The official reply was that The Queen had been 'very interested' in the contents of the letter, but that it would be 'most regrettable' to connect Her Majesty to something that could turn out to be a hoax. It was also not felt 'generally very appropriate' to name the possible creature after The Queen, as it had been nicknamed the Monster

We have to give you what?

Great Yarmouth, Norfolk, must provide 100 herrings baked into 24 pasties to the Sherriff, who passes them along to the Sovereign

The owner of Sauchlemuir Castle must pour three glasses of Port on New Year's Eve (for the grandmother of James IV)

The City of Gloucester pays for its holdings of Crown Lands in the form of a large lamphrey pie

Hungerford, Berkshire, must pay The Queen for its fishing and grazing rights with a single red rose

Other famous people born in 1926

- ▸ **Moira Shearer** (January 17) ▸ **Leslie Nielsen** (February 11)
- ▸ **Kenneth Williams** (February 22) ▸ **Jerry Lewis** (March 16)
- ▸ **Hugh Hefner** (April 9) ▸ **Miles Davis** (May 26)
- ▸ **Marilyn Monroe** (June 1) ▸ **Lionel Jeffries** (June 10)
- ▸ **Mel Brooks** (June 28) ▸ **Tony Bennett** (August 3)
- ▸ **Fidel Castro** (August 13)
- ▸ **John Coltrane** (September 23)
- ▸ **Joan Sutherland** (November 7)

Sitting room only: crowds wait for a glimpse of the newly married royal couple in 1947

Meeting the people

More than 400,000 honours
and awards conferred

———

Royal Assent given to more than
3,500 Acts of Parliament

———

In 2017–18, the Sovereign Grant
(£45.7 million) paid for:
- More than 400 staff
- 97 receptions, 43 lunches,
7 garden parties and 56 dinners
at Buckingham Palace, Windsor Castle,
St James's Palace and Holyroodhouse
- Official journeys of the
Royal Family, attending more than
3,000 engagements
- Maintenance and re-servicing of royal
residences (the usual funding is not
enough to cover the refurbishment of
Buckingham Palace as it's so extensive,
so Parliament approved a 10-year
increase in the Sovereign Grant.
Instead of 15% of the Crown Estate's
profits, the Sovereign Grant would
take 25%. In 2017–18, that amounted
to £30.4 million)

Queen of Arts

The Queen sat for more than 135 portraits during her reign, painted in a variety of styles. Her first portrait was made in 1933, when she was seven

―――――

The National Portrait Gallery has 967 images associated with her

―――――

She has been portrayed as a character in about 100 films and TV series, including *The Crown, The Queen* and *A Question of Attribution*

―――――

She became a Bond Girl in 2012, when she appeared with Daniel Craig in a short film for the opening ceremony of the London Olympics. Appearing to parachute into the venue, she made her entrance and enjoyed the faces of her astonished family

―――――

She had quite a gift for mimicry. According to the Associated Press, her chaplain Bishop Michael Mann once said that 'The Queen imitating Concorde landing is one of the funniest things you could see'

Top: Dame Helen Mirren in *The Queen*, with Michael Sheen as Tony Blair. *Left:* Dame Penelope Wilton saving the day in *The BFG. Above:* Claire Foy in *The Crown*

Money, money, money

The image of Elizabeth II appears on the coinage of at least 35 different countries, more than any other monarch in her lifetime. That means, as some two billion new coins are struck for the UK alone each year, her portrait has travelled more widely and been reproduced more times than anyone else's

The face on UK coinage has been updated five times (*above*). Coins using the first portrait, by Mary Gillick, were minted until decimalisation in 1971, followed by:
1971–85 portrait by Arnold Machin
1985–97 portrait by Raphael Maklouf
1997–2015 portrait by Ian Rank-Broadley
Since 2015 portrait by Jody Clark

Banknotes and coins bearing the head of the new King were prepared ahead of his accession and made available immediately upon The Queen's death. We will still be able to see Elizabeth II on our money for a while, however, as notes won't be withdrawn until they're damaged or soiled—because there are 211 million £5 notes alone in circulation at any one time, it would be impossible to do otherwise

The Bank of Canada issued a $20 note in 1935, featuring a portrait of the then Princess Elizabeth when she was eight

More than a figurehead

Thanks to television and air travel, Elizabeth II was more visible than any other monarch, but it was her personal touch that cemented the unbreakable bond with her people

Written by Clive Aslet

ON June 7, 1977, Britain put aside fears of imminent national bankruptcy to throw 12,000 street parties. One million people crowded the streets of London to watch The Queen pass by in a golden coach. A further 500 million subjects across the Commonwealth followed the day on television. This was the Silver Jubilee.

Initial thoughts of downplaying it by the Callaghan government were put aside in the hope that it would provide a grand, patriotic distraction from the chaos of the times. It was a sound decision. The sun shone

between sudden downpours; campers outside St Paul's Cathedral, determined to get a good view of The Queen as she attended a service of thanksgiving, climbed into black-plastic bin liners to avoid the showers. However, such rain as there was (nothing compared with the Diamond Jubilee, 35 years later) couldn't dampen the spirits. Flags were waved, Union Flag hats and aprons donned, bonfires lit.

In her Christmas speech that year, The Queen reflected on the scene: 'The street parties and village fêtes, the presents, the flowers from the children, the mile upon

mile of decorated streets and houses: these things suggest that the real value and pleasure of the celebration was that we all shared in it together.'

It happened again in 2002. Beforehand, the Eeyores of the hour had done their best to disparage it. 'The Queen's advisers must be a naïve lot if they were really expecting as much public enthusiasm for Her ➤

Above: Crowds throng the Mall to celebrate the Golden Jubilee. *Facing page:* A radiant Queen Elizabeth pictured on her journey to the State Opening of Parliament in 1971

She has two great assets.
First of all, she sleeps
very well and, secondly,
she's got very good legs
and she can stand
for a long time...
The Queen is as tough
as a yak

One of Her Majesty's private secretaries explains
the key to a successful walkabout

Majesty's Golden Jubilee as there was for her Silver,' wrote a correspondent to *The Times* that January. 'Since 1977, the reputation of the Royal Family has suffered a catastrophic decline', the result of which would be 'apathy, indifference and even antagonism'.

Red tape would strangle the street parties, planned with the aid of a 35-page booklet issued by the Golden Jubilee Office; the 'celebrations toolkit' recommended that organisers should buy an Events Safety Guide published by the Health and Safety Executive at a cost of £20. However, as so often, the doomsayers were confounded. Months of receptions, garden parties, concerts and more than 50 walkabouts culminated in four days of celebration.

For the first time, the gardens of Buckingham Palace became a concert venue, earning The Queen a gold disc from the recording industry when 100,000 copies of the *Party at the Palace* CD were sold within the first week of release.

The finale of the Jubilee weekend included a flypast of 27 aircraft, led by the tubby RAF C-17 Globemaster heavy-lift transport and ending with a svelte, paper dart-shaped Concorde and the Red Arrows trailing red, white and blue. Two and a half tons of fireworks were launched from the roof of the Palace and the grounds of Green Park.

The biting squalls that accompanied the Diamond Jubilee are still too fresh in the memory to dwell on, but the bunting had been bought and no amount of cruel weather would stop the street parties from being staged to mark it; an estimated 8.5 million people took part in Big Jubilee Lunches.

Nor could anything deter the brilliantly conceived Thames Pageant, at which The Queen and the Duke of Edinburgh stood adamantine at the prow of the Royal Barge, figureheads in every sense of the word, at the head of 1,000 boats from across the UK and around the world. More than one million people assembled to watch it.

It hasn't been often—at 25, 50 and 60 years—that the British public has had the opportunity to come together to express its love and gratitude to The Queen for her years of service, but, when the chance came along, we seized it with both hands.

Yes, there are some of other persuasion. In 1977, the Silver Jubilee inspired the Sex Pistols to charter a boat named *Queen Elizabeth*, the voyage of which was intended to mock a royal river procession that was to take place a couple of days later. It was immediately surrounded by police vessels and, as night fell, several people were arrested. However, the anarchic *God Save the Queen* —is song the right word for it?—made the

No 2 position on the UK Singles Chart: a reflection of republican sentiment at the time.

In 2018, such views seem to have weakened, with opinion polls showing more than 70% support for the monarchy and an expectation that it could help rally the country after Brexit. Much of this was due to the example of The Queen herself. What had made her so popular?

Longevity is one answer. Only the elderly can remember a time when she was not on the throne and, in all her long reign, in contrast with other institutions, she had barely been touched by scandal in any form and her dedication to duty was recognised by all, even her detractors.

Although The Queen's life may not have been—indeed, could not have been—the same as other people's, her instincts were. This was seen early. When still a girl, during the Second World War, she was anxious to join the Women's Auxiliary Territorial Service, despite her father's misgivings. She enjoyed the experience, which made her a fast, confident driver.

Decades later, a glimpse of the Royal Family's home life was caught by the television cameras for *Royal Family*, which ➤

followed them for more than a year, before being aired in 1969. This showed her tastes to be almost radically normal: her downtime was spent as a country lady, who made the salad herself and stored food in Tupperware containers. Although they had the royal kitchens at their disposal, both she and the Duke of Edinburgh preferred to eat simply when they were alone. (Having been watched by three-quarters of the UK population, the film was never shown again; there was only so much normality the public was thought capable of taking.)

Elizabeth II's long reign also coincided with a technological revolution in terms of both travel and media. In February 1952, jet planes were still something of a novelty: the world's first scheduled service by one didn't take place until later that year. Thus, it was symbolic of the new age that The Queen's first step back onto British soil as sovereign should have taken place at London Airport (now Heathrow), as she descended from the BOAC Canadair Argonaut airliner *Atalanta*, which had brought her home from Uganda.

Faster planes, covering longer distances: the jet engine enabled The Queen to visit more of the Commonwealth than any previous head of state had seen of the Empire. Tours became a near-annual fixture, taking in Jamaica, Fiji, Tonga, New Zealand, Australia, the Cocos Islands, Ceylon, Aden, Malta, Nigeria and Canada in the 1950s alone and numerous other destinations covering almost all the globe since.

Many people acquired their first television set for the Coronation. Initially, there was some reluctance to show the ceremony as it took place in Westminster Abbey, but the Coronation Commission, headed by the Duke of Edinburgh, reversed the initial decision not to allow cameras east of the organ screen.

To ensure that the broadcast reached the extremities of the nation, previously unblessed with the requisite signal, the Postmaster General gave the order that transmitters (makeshift affairs, seated in old outside-broadcast vans) would be built in Co Durham and the Belfast Hills.

'Gratitude, respect and pride... sum up how I feel about the people of this country'

Elizabeth II on her Golden Jubilee

Preceding pages: A light display beamed onto the façade of Buckingham Palace echoes the sentiment of the jubilant crowd. *Above:* A bittersweet day: the new Queen arrives back in the UK from Uganda in 1952

In Britain, it was estimated that more than 20 million people tuned in. There being fewer than three million television sets in the country, the figures meant that 7.8 million watched in their own homes, 10.4 million in other people's homes and 1.5 million in cinemas, halls and pubs.

Television, then 30 years old, was given a boost, helping it on the inexorable rise that would make it the dominant news medium of the later 20th century. By 1960, Buckingham Palace alone owned 50 sets (royal palaces being exempt from the licence fee). Her Majesty's taste for Gracie Fields, Morecambe and Wise, *Dad's Army* and wrestling on *World of Sport* was one that she shared with the population at large.

Initially, The Queen herself had been reluctant to allow the moment of her coronation to be televised and yet the result, following a change of mind, raised enthusiasm for the monarchy to a new high. Through the flickering, grainy images, the nation could see a great human drama being lived ➤

'I cannot lead you into
battle, I do not give you
laws or administer
justice, but I can do
something else,
I can give you my heart
and my devotion to these
old islands and to all
the peoples of our
brotherhood of nations'

—————

Christmas Message, 1957

Country Life Commemorative Issue

out, as a lovely young woman assumed the responsibilities of the highest power in the land, accompanied by all the pomp of which the British constitution is capable.

Later, it might occasionally have seemed that Her Majesty's initial instincts were correct. Television would prove a Pandora's box for the Royal Family: once opened, its demons would fly everywhere, with an increasing disregard for the constraints that would once have been imposed by deference. However, it also enabled the image of The Queen to be projected into living rooms across Britain with an intimacy unavailable to previous monarchs.

'I very much hope this new medium will make my message more personal and direct,' Her Majesty said in her first televised Christmas Day broadcast, made in 1957. 'It is inevitable that I should seem a rather remote figure to many of you... but now, at least for a few minutes, I welcome you to the peace of my own home.'

'If I wore beige, nobody would know who I am'

A very modest monarch

Nothing can beat the effect of a personal encounter with the sovereign, however distant: a piece of royal PR lore passed down from the age of the Tudors. The strain of smiling and waving for an extended period is not inconsiderable—the facial muscles twitch, the hand aches, but The Queen smiled and waved because subjects who had travelled far to see her would have been disappointed if she had not.

In 1970, she brought a new word into the language with 'walkabout'; her first was in New Zealand, with the experiment being quickly repeated in Coventry. Actually talking to The Queen reduced many people to a state of blathering idiocy. Never mind— it was an experience they would never forget.

So assiduous has been the walking about, the waving and the constant 'Have you come far' that it seemed as much as one-third of the UK population might have either met The Queen or seen her in person. As celebrity culture replaces deference, she retained the lustre not only of a royal, but of an icon. Britain loved her for it. ➤

Paddington Bear came to tea to mark Her Majesty's Platinum Jubilee and we finally found out what The Queen kept in her handbag—a marmalade sandwich, of course

Riding in the Gold State Coach with
The Duke of Edinburgh in the parade from
Buckingham Palace to St Paul's Cathedral
to celebrate the Golden Jubilee in 2002.
Designed by William Chambers and made
by Samuel Butler, the gilded coach was
commissioned for the coronation of George III
in 1761 and is drawn by eight grey horses

A little princess

Princess Elizabeth's idyllic childhood was shattered by her father's unexpected ascension to the throne, but she had been in the spotlight all around the world from the moment of her birth

Written by Matthew Dennison

EXPECTATIONS were conventional for the princess born on April 21, 1926, and christened a month later, in the private chapel of Buckingham Palace, Elizabeth Alexandra Mary. They did not include sovereignty.

Nevertheless, the first-born child of Albert, Duke of York, George V's second son, found herself, from the moment of her birth, third in line to the grandest throne in Europe and a source of considerable interest at home and across the Empire.

Her first inheritance was neither thrones nor dominions, but a nurse—her mother's former nurse, Clara Knight, nicknamed Allah. With Allah, she shared the nursery of the London town house, 145, Piccadilly, into which her parents moved in 1927. With Allah, the baby princess enjoyed excursions to Hyde Park, exciting such curiosity among passers-by that the King, a surprisingly doting grandfather, ordered a landau from the Royal Mews to replace the gleaming perambulator. From the outset, Elizabeth lived her life in the public gaze.

Until the birth of her sister, Margaret Rose, in August 1930, she was an only child. Overseas tours separated her from her parents: she spent considerable periods with her formidable grandparents, George V and Queen Mary. It was the King—brusque and dismissive towards other children, including his own—who called her Lilibet, copying her own first attempts to pronounce her name. It was also the King who, on her fourth birthday, gave Elizabeth her first pony, a Shetland called Peggy, weeks after her first riding lesson, with Col A. E. Erskine, a Crown Equerry.

Both the Duke and Duchess of York (the future George VI and Queen Elizabeth) were devoted parents and the family life of 'us four'—the Duke's description—was markedly happy. Weekends were spent at Royal Lodge in Windsor Great Park, there

A jolly little girl, but fundamentally sensible and well behaved

Margaret Rhodes, Elizabeth's cousin

Above: Princess Elizabeth Alexandra Mary, when she was nearly one year old. *Facing page:* Y Bwythyn Bach at Royal Lodge, Windsor, was a gift from the Welsh people on Elizabeth's sixth birthday and has recently been refurbished by Princess Beatrice

were ponies and gardening, songs around the piano, comic novels by P. G. Wodehouse, a miniature house in which to play (Y Bwythyn Bach, a gift from the people of Wales) and, from 1933, the first of a long line of beloved corgis.

No plans were made to send the princesses to school. Following the arrival, in the spring of 1932, of a youthful Scots governess Marion Crawford, known as Crawfie, lessons took place in the upstairs schoolroom.

Initially, Elizabeth's timetable was light. Crawfie explained its shortcomings as arising from the royal parents' wish that ➤

both their daughters have 'a really happy childhood, with lots of pleasant memories'.

Queen Mary did her best to balance this lack of rigour: she took her granddaughters to sites of historic and, especially, royal interest, determined to impress upon them her own view of the sanctity and splendour of monarchy. Appropriately deferential press reports include a description of Elizabeth aged nine as 'happy-natured but serious and quaintly dignified'.

> # We are so anxious for her first name to be Elizabeth as it is such a nice name and there has been no one of that name in your family for a long time... Elizabeth of York sounds so nice too
>
> The Duke of York writes to George V

In December 1936, the straightforward ease of Elizabeth's childhood ended abruptly. Her unmarried uncle David, Edward VIII, abdicated within a year of his accession. The Duke of York became king by default. With his family, he moved into Buckingham Palace three months ahead of his Coronation.

Elizabeth was 10 years old and was rewarded with a sitting room of her own. She no longer had any doubts about her destiny. To add a note of normality to what remained of her childhood, a Girl Guide troop, the 1st Buckingham Palace Company, was formed for her, but meals in the nursery were served by footmen in scarlet livery and both Elizabeth and Margaret curtseyed to their parents.

Her father's unexpected accession had changed Elizabeth's world irrevocably. Under the watchful eye of Queen Mary, both princesses took part in their parents' Coronation in May 1937: Elizabeth described it as 'very, very wonderful'.

At Christmas, she attended a children's performance of *Where the Rainbow Ends*. A specially composed children's verse of the National Anthem, sung to her by the audience of 1,500 children, impressed on

Top: The Duchess of York arrives at Olympia for the Royal Tournament in 1935, with her two daughters, Margaret (*centre*) and Elizabeth (*right*). *Above:* Aleady a promising horsewoman, in Windsor Great Park in 1939. She was given her first pony, Peggy, when she was four

Above left: Learning the duties expected of a monarch. *Above right:* January 31, 1952, was the last time Princess Elizabeth would see her father—six days after she left for Africa, he was dead. *Below:* 'Us four'—a happy family, inevitably accompanied by assorted dogs

her as forcefully as the service in Westminster Abbey her altered circumstances and her destiny.

Having been unprepared himself for kingship, the new George VI began to ready his daughter for the path ahead. Twice a week, Henry Marten, vice-provost of Eton College, gave Elizabeth lessons in constitutional history; the Vicomtesse de Bellaigue taught both sisters French conversation and European history.

Elizabeth embarked on her first royal duties, becoming president of the Princess Elizabeth of York Hospital Children's League on her 13th birthday, in 1939. That summer, on a family visit to the Royal Naval College Dartmouth, she was reintroduced to a distant cousin, Prince Philip of Greece.

With the outbreak of war, Elizabeth and Margaret were evacuated to Windsor Castle, where nursery and schoolroom routines continued as previously. After announcements, following her 18th birthday, that Elizabeth would work in a munitions factory or join the women's services, she was gazetted as Second Subaltern in the Auxiliary Territorial Services and posted to No 1 Mechanical Transport Training Centre, a position she relished. In July, anticipating things to come, her father appointed her Counsellor of State. ✎

Acknowledging the cheering
crowds at her father's Coronation
on May 12, 1937

God save The Queen!

For the first time, a sovereign's Coronation was televised, affording the public
a glimpse of the young Queen amid dazzling pomp and pagentry

Written by Matthew Dennison

FOR readers of *The Coronation Book of Queen Elizabeth II,* a glossy, hardback commemorative published hot on the heels of the first televised royal ceremonial spectacular, the Bishop of Bath and Wells explained what sovereignty meant for new Elizabethans. 'It is a vocation to a sacred office, which demands not only popular acclaim, and constitutional sanction, but also the outward and visible signs of a Divine call, of the grace and favour of God, and of a personal dedication to the service of God.'

Undoubtedly, Britain's 27-year-old new sovereign agreed. At the heart of the ancient service at Westminster Abbey was a promise made by a serious-minded young woman of deep Christian faith to the God in whom her belief was firm. That promise echoed the speech made on her 21st birthday,

in which she had dedicated herself lifelong to British and Commonwealth service.

Amid glittering flummery of the utmost gorgeousness—the splendour of medieval majesty reinvented for a Technicolour age by Norman Hartnell and beamed, through the still novel medium of television, into sitting rooms the length and breadth of the kingdom—Elizabeth II's self-sacrifice to duty proved deeply moving.

She sealed her promises with a kiss on the Bible on the altar and, in St Edward's Chair, under a canopy held by Garter Knights, was anointed by the Archbishop of Canterbury: the sign of the cross drawn on both her palms, on the crown of her head and on her breast. She received the royal regalia, including the orb and sceptre: the Archbishop placed on her head St Edward's Crown of gold, pearls and precious stones

—at almost 5lb, its physical weight was a reminder of the burden placed upon her.

On a throne on a dais, she received the homage of the Archbishop of Canterbury, a trio of royal dukes—including her husband, the Duke of Edinburgh—and the nation's senior duke, marquess, earl, viscount and baron. For the service's final flourish, in St Edward's Chapel, The Queen exchanged St Edward's Crown for the Imperial State Crown, the most dazzling of royal jewels, which she subsequently wore annually for the State Opening of Parliament. ➤

Above: On seeing his wife for the first time after her Coronation, Prince Philip joked irrepressibly: 'Where did you get that hat?' *Facing page:* Elizabeth II, photographed by Cecil Beaton, was the sixth Queen to be crowned at Westminster in her own right

Above: Tiaras may be worn: a diamond setter examines an exquisite tiara at the Goldsmiths' and Silversmiths' Company in London's Regent Street. *Below:* A banner day: artists hard at work creating royal flags and standards at Edgington's factory in Sidcup, Kent

Above: Crowds watch the Commonwealth detatchments go through Admiralty Arch. *Facing page:* Adding heavy gold braid to Household Cavalry uniforms at Messrs L. Silverton. *Facing page, far right:* Seymour Joly de Lotbinière, head of the BBC's outside-broadcast team, directs mobile units from Broadcasting House

'The Coronation was like a phoenix-time… nothing to stop anything getting better and better'

Princess Margaret

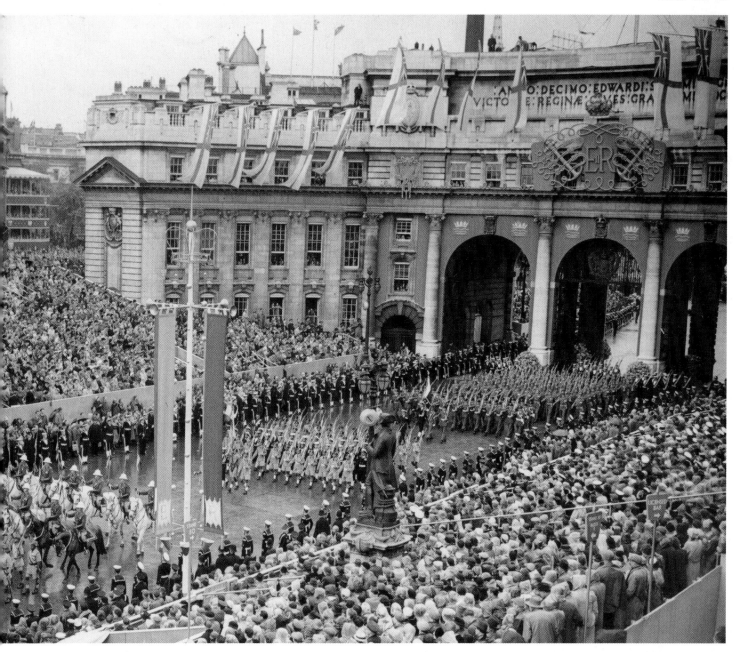

Above: The newly crowned Queen processes out of Westminster Abbey. *Below:* Prince Charles told a BBC documentary: 'I remember my Mama coming, you know, up, when we were bathed as children, wearing the crown. It was quite funny—practising'

However, the Coronation of Elizabeth II, on a day of steel-grey drizzle in June 1953, 16 months after her accession, was not exclusively concerned with the weighty business of duty, as the congregation of 7,500 packed into the Abbey and a global television audience of millions was quick to realise.

Once the Palace had agreed the service be televised, the pressure to produce a perfect piece of pageantry mounted. Understandably, the new Queen concerned herself with her own part in the service's elaborate choreography, her clothes and her management of heavy jewels and a lengthy train. She was determined her Coronation gown enhance the beauty of the occasion and nothing so trivial as wardrobe difficulties would mar the single most important day of her life.

To design her Coronation dresses, The Queen chose couturier Norman Hartnell, who, six years earlier, had designed her wedding dress, complete with embroidery of 10,000 pearls and a full Court train. His instructions were for a dress of similar outline, made in white satin.

Hartnell produced eight sketches. His own favourite was also The Queen's: a silver- and crystal-embroidered dress featuring the flower emblems of the UK. The Queen requested the addition of floral emblems of the Dominions. The Garter King of Arms insisted the leek replace the daffodil as the emblem of Wales; a horrified Hartnell agreed.

Opals, pearls and crystals studded a skirt so heavy that it was necessary to support it with a lining of pale taffeta and a crinoline constructed of several layers of horsehair. On this framework, it moved with a gentle, bell-like sway that appeared to spectators to emphasise The Queen's dignity. 'As she walks,' declared Cecil Beaton, 'she allows her heavy skirt to swing backwards and forwards in a beautiful rhythmic effect.'

It was no accident. On her accession, The Queen—with the Duke of Edinburgh, Prince Charles and baby Princess Anne—had moved into first- and second-floor apartments on the north side of Buckingham Palace's central quadrangle, with the royal nursery on the floor above. These rooms were not large enough for her to practise Coronation ceremonial and she rehearsed instead in the State Ballroom, sheets attached to her shoulders to suggest the weight of her robes.

Fifteen years earlier, she had watched her father practise wearing St Edward's Crown, a preparation she assiduously copied.

No one watching noticed a handful of tiny glitches in proceedings. Instead, their attention was riveted by an intensely serious young woman, in the prime of her beauty, embracing a historic destiny. ✦

'As this day draws
to a close, I know that
my abiding memory
of it will not only be the
solemnity and beauty
of the ceremony, but the
inspiration of your
loyalty and affection'

Radio broadcast to the nation on the
evening of the Coronation

A solemn vow: the newly crowned Monarch—wearing the Imperial State Crown—holds the Sovereign's Sceptre, symbolising temporal power, and the Sovereign's Sceptre with Dove. The white dove of the latter represents the Holy Spirit and the sceptre is traditionally known as the Rod of Equity and Mercy

A lasting love

Elizabeth II made two lifelong commitments: to her country and to her husband. Both involved sacrifice, but both brought her joy

Written by Jane Watkins

E'VE all been read the fairy tale: handsome prince meets beautiful girl and they fall in love at first sight, before living happily ever after. Once we grow up, we know that it's never as simple as that and we realise how rare such a commitment can be. For The Queen and the Duke of Edinburgh, their story didn't begin with a glass slipper or a wicked fairy's curse, but their lasting devotion was, nonetheless, something worth the telling.

And lasting it indeed was, as well as historic. The Queen is the first British monarch to have celebrated a diamond and blue-sapphire wedding anniversary and, very like her astonishingly long reign, it's a feat that's unlikely to be matched.

Speaking at a lunch to celebrate her golden wedding at Banqueting House in November 1997, she made clear some of the depth of her feeling about the Duke: 'He has, quite simply, been my strength and stay all these years and I, and his whole family, and this and many other countries, owe him a debt greater than he would ever claim, or we shall ever know.'

Toasting his wife, the Duke's affectionate tribute was: 'I think the main lesson that we have learnt is that tolerance is the one essential ingredient of any happy marriage. It may not be quite so important when things are going well, but it is absolutely vital when the going gets difficult. You can take it from me that The Queen has the quality of tolerance in abundance.'

Others have a clear view of what made their partnership a lasting and strong one. 'Prince Philip is the only man in the world who treats The Queen simply as another human being,' stated Lord Charteris, Her Majesty's former private secretary.

'Millions will welcome this joyous event as a flash of colour on the hard road we have to travel'

Winston Churchill

One of the couple's grandsons, The Duke of Cambridge, went further in 2012, explaining admiringly: 'He makes her laugh because of some of the things he says and does and the way he looks at life

A true look of love: the affection between the royal couple was always clear, no matter how long they had been together

is obviously slightly different than her, so, together, they're a great couple.'

Their first meeting was hardly auspicious. In 1934, they attended the wedding of Prince Philip's cousin, Princess Marina of Greece and Denmark, and Elizabeth's uncle, Prince George, Duke of Kent. Elizabeth was eight years old and Philip 14.

In July 1939, the Royal Family visited the Royal Naval College in Dartmouth. Because two of the other cadets had contracted mumps, Philip was the only one allowed to meet them. Sir John Wheeler-Bennett, George VI's official biographer, said the Princess immediately fell for the handsome 18 year old: 'This was the man with whom Princess Elizabeth had been in love from their first meeting.'

Marion Crawford, Elizabeth's governess, recalled the day less rosily: 'I thought he showed off a good deal.' It was clear, however, that the Princess had been impressed with his jumping over the tennis nets and 'never took her eyes off him the whole time', gushing to her governess: 'How good he is, Crawfie. How high he can jump.' ➤

Facing page: Always in step: in November 1947, the newly married couple wave to the press pack on the first part of their honeymoon at Lord Mountbatten's Broadlands House in Hampshire. They then travelled to Birkhall Lodge on the Balmoral estate. *Top:* A loving glance at Trooping the Colour. *Above left:* Sir Winston Churchill echoed the feelings of a nation in his wish 'that they may find true happiness together and be guided on the paths of duty and honour'. *Above right:* Sharing a joke and a blanket at the Braemar Gathering ➤

The two began to correspond and, to allay any gossip about their relationship, the Princess replaced the photograph of a clean-shaven Philip she kept in her room with one of him sporting a large beard.

Although they were separated by the Second World War and its aftermath, the couple's feelings for each other remained undimmed. They began to talk of an engagement, but the King asked his daughter to wait until she returned from a tour of South Africa with her parents. He was worried that Elizabeth was too young to make such a commitment. However, he liked Philip enormously, writing to his mother that the young man was 'intelligent, has a good sense of humour and thinks about things in the right way'.

There was a great deal of opposition to the match. His family was thought impossible: his mother had been institutionalised in Switzerland and his sisters were married to aristocratic Germans who were also high-ranking Nazis.

Elizabeth could not, however, be swayed from her real-life prince charming and the engagement was, finally, announced on July 9, 1947, although they had become secretly bethrothed on her 21st birthday, Philip reportedly proposing during a walk around the grounds of Balmoral. Elizabeth declared: 'I ask nothing more than that Philip and I should be as happy as my father and mother have been, and Queen Mary and King George before them.'

According to Philip Eade, author of *Young Prince Philip: His Turbulent Early Life*, Philip wrote to Princess Elizabeth shortly afterwards: 'To have been spared in the war and seen victory, to have been given the chance to rest and to re-adjust myself, to have fallen in love completely and unreservedly, makes all one's personal and even the world's troubles seem small and petty.'

Designed by the groom to be, the platinum engagement ring was made by jeweller Philip Antrobus, using diamonds from a tiara that had been given to Princess Alice, Philip's mother, on her wedding day. The ring—which features a three-carat, round-cut diamond centre stone as well as 10 smaller ones—

may have been relatively modest for the heiress to the throne, but perfectly matched the prevailing mood of post-war austerity.

Writing to her parents afterwards, the Princess described the couple's close bond: 'We behave as though we had belonged to each other for years. Philip is an angel—he is so kind and thoughtful.' She expressed her wishes for their future, too: 'I only hope that I can bring up my children in the happy atmosphere of love and fairness which Margaret and I have grown up in.'

For his part, George VI made it clear that he finally approved of her choice, writing: 'Your leaving us has left a great blank in our lives. But do remember that your old home is still yours and do come back to it as much and as often as possible. I can see that you are sublimely happy with Philip which is

Below: To mark their 60th anniversary, the Duke surprised The Queen with a return trip to Broadlands, in an echo of their happy honeymoon. *Facing page:* Two different personalities, but one formidable team

right but don't forget us, is the wish of your ever loving and devoted… Papa.'

Philip was no less certain of their bond, writing to Queen Elizabeth: 'Cherish Lilibet? I wonder if that word is enough to express what is in me.' He declared his new wife was 'the only thing in this world which is absolutely real to me and my ambition is to weld the two of us into a new combined existence that will not only be able to withstand the shocks directed at us but will also have a positive existence for the good'.

Although sometimes chafing at being relegated to 'a bloody amoeba', the Duke accompanied and supported his wife for many decades until he retired from public duties. He would often think ahead to ensure that official engagements ran as smoothly as possible, for example, ensuring she had a pen if one hadn't been provided.

Although he became known for what the press insisted were 'gaffes', he saw it as his job to make the people who were waiting for The Queen laugh, so that she only saw smiling faces, rather than anxious ones. Prosaically, he declared: 'My job first, second and last is never to let The Queen down.'

Although they both came from a generation that eschewed public displays of affection, the love between them was always clear in the way The Queen looked up towards her husband or little gestures he made during walkabouts to delight her, such as pulling small children out of the crowds with gifts to present.

'I, Philip, Duke of Edinburgh do become your liege man of life and limb and of earthly worship'

The Duke swears his allegiance

A sea change in the way in which the Royal Family was presented to the public in the early part of this century also gave a more relaxed view of the couple. Biographies and television interviews revealed choice tidbits, such as the Duke reportedly calling his wife 'Cabbage'.

The couple both had fiery tempers, but the stories of flaming rows are few and far between because they knew they were better together. 'They are different people. Yet they understand one another. Completely. And they are allies,' declared author Gyles Brandreth, who examined their relationship in *Philip & Elizabeth: Portrait of a Marriage.*

As their granddaughter Princess Eugenie put it: 'Together, they are invincible.'

Surely no one would cavil at the description of the marriage of The Queen and the Duke as truly the romance of the century. When he died a few months before his 100th birthday, there was no sadder sight than The Queen sitting alone, due to Covid restrictions, to mourn her beloved husband.

The Queen and The Duke of Edinburgh
attend a dinner at Clarence House
in London to celebrate their diamond
wedding anniversary with their children:
Prince Charles (who was born in 1948),
Prince Andrew (born 1960), Princess Anne
(born 1950) and Prince Edward (born 1964)

Home is where the heart is

The family has been at the centre of The Queen's life since her idyllic childhood and it has been her mainstay throughout the years

Written by Clive Aslet

I T'S impossible to think of The Queen without her family. Collectively, they are 'the Firm' and one of her universally recognised strengths, together with a dedication to service, has been her devotion to family: both the Royal Family as actors in the national drama and her husband and children at home.

Such behind-the-scenes glimpses of Her Majesty's private life, as have escaped into the media from time to time, showed a countrywoman whose greatest relaxation was the domestic existence that her schedule so often denied her: days spent with family,

dogs and horses. Even today, the Royal Family personifies the greater family of the British nation.

This is a relatively modern conception of monarchy. It can be traced to Queen Victoria, whose life was shaped by the intensity of her love for Prince Albert. 'They say no Sovereign was more loved than I am,' she wrote in a letter of 1844; her popularity derived 'from our happy domestic home—which gives such a good example'. Her rackety, spendthrift uncles—two of them kings—had hardly been so respectable. Nor would the Prince of Wales, Edward VII, be.

However, his gruff successor, George V, was, by nature, a family man, often being photographed with his sons, the future Edward VIII and George VI, whether in uniform or shooting. As a father, he was harsh, pursuing a parenting style that spectacularly failed to work with the elder boy, who preferred a playboy lifestyle to the responsibilities that he had inherited. Edward's ➤

Above: The documentary *Royal Family* showed the public The Queen's day-to-day life. *Facing page:* She always tried to replicate her own idyllic childhood as far as she could

determination to marry the twice-divorced American Wallis Simpson led, swiftly, to the Abdication in December 1936. It was a searing experience that affected members of the Royal Family then and afterwards and they never forgot it.

Fortunately, his naturally shy brother, George VI, was happy in his marriage, with two daughters whom the public took to its heart. Although the period of George VI's reign was unusually turbulent, with the Second World War and its aftermath, including the loss of India, his own image provided an effective foil. He rejoiced in being homely. It put him in communion with his subjects.

'I was so proud of you & thrilled at having you so close to me on your long walk in Westminster Abbey,' wrote the King to his newly married daughter, Princess Elizabeth, when she was on her honeymoon with Prince Philip. 'I have watched you grow up all these years with pride under the skilful direction of Mummy, who, as you know is the most marvellous person in the World in my eyes.'

For a man who was not outwardly emotional, this was a touching expression of feelings that any parent might have on such an occasion, allowing for the difference in circumstances, and the King's confidence would be fully justified by events. Following her accession, The Queen continued the

course set by her father, in emphasising that family is the mainstay not only of monarchy, but of this monarch in particular.

The pomp of majesty was adopted for occasions of state, but her own tastes, as were those of Prince Philip, were naturally simple and, judged by the opulent standards of 21st-century billionaires, frugal.

'A thoroughly close-knit and happy family, all wrapped up in each other'

Gen Sir Alan Brooke, Chief of the Imperial General Staff

However, the mission of projecting the Royal Family as a microcosm of all families in the land was fraught. Even in the 1950s, it was obvious that the royals operated on a different plane. Half a century earlier, Edward VII followed much the same life as the aristocracy, in a social circle that contained financiers and other *nouveaux riche*; he was far from being the richest of his set.

After the Second World War, The Queen, deeply conservative in domestic matters, continued to live as her grandfather and

The Queen was a constant for Princes William and Harry as the Waleses' marriage crumbled

father had lived, attended by footmen, as the contemporaries who should have been her near equals fell away. This happened against the background of a wider social change. Post-war Socialism was followed by the revolution in attitudes that occurred during the Swinging Sixties. The Royal Family was out on a limb.

An attempt to bridge the divide was made in 1969, when Her Majesty was counselled to overcome her instinctive reserve by allowing a film to be made. Called simply *Royal Family*, it followed The Queen on duty and at home. 'The overwhelming impression given by the film was of a woman happy and busy in her public and private life,' wrote her biographer Sarah Bradford, 'enjoying her job as much as she did the company of her four children.'

Life for The Queen and The Duke of Edinburgh could appear antediluvian—at Buckingham Palace, the kitchen might be 200 yards from the place where they ate a modest lunch—but The Queen's naturalness made her a star and the family's devotion to outdoor pursuits, preferably in Scotland, seemed no more than charmingly old-fashioned.

Today, the dangers of the exercise seem obvious. No family is perfect all the time and the film established a yardstick by which this one would be judged when the marriages of the younger generation went wrong. Rather than satisfying a public appetite for curiosity, it only left the prurient wanting more.

Three years earlier, the journalist Leonard Mosely had written a thin book called *The Royals*. In it, he analysed the marriage prospects of The Prince of Wales with what seems chilling prescience. 'It seems to have escaped the notice of most people who write criticising the Royal Family and speculating on the future of the Monarchy that, in a year or two, the future King of England will fall in love and take a bride, though the two events will not necessarily coincide in time nor concern the same person…

'Though moral values have changed, standards are different, attitudes are awry, it still seems more than likely that the bride of The Prince of Wales will be chosen for him rather than picked by him, and that the pulse-beat of national interest rather than the heartbeat of passion will decide the choice.'

History would reveal the impossibility of finding a bride who—even if she came from the upper reaches of the aristocracy—understood marriage in this outmoded way. Faultlines opened not only in Prince Charles's marriage, but in those of two of his siblings. The result, added to the fire at

Windsor Castle, was what Her Majesty, the last person to wear her feelings on her sleeve, described as her '*annus horribilis*'.

How long ago it now seems. Penance has been paid. Above all, The Queen's unwavering commitment to her belief in the family won sympathy and admiration. The 1969 film successfully presented the royals as a family like other families. This was, at best, only a partial truth. By the standards of most people, they're odd and must always remain so, but a quarter of a century of social evolution has shown that plenty of other people, by old-fashioned standards, are equally as odd, if not odder.

Odd is the new normal. Marital breakdown has become commonplace. The public grieves for the disasters that it sees being played out in the life of the Royal Family, followed with the avidity of a boxset (indeed, many confuse the plotlines of *The Crown* with the real thing). However, many people can identify with them through their own experience; fewer people are willing to cast the first stone.

When *Royal Family* was in the making, David Attenborough made an analogy with anthropology. 'The whole institution depends on mystique and the tribal chief in his hut,' he wrote to its producer-director, Richard Cawston. 'If any member of the tribe ever sees inside the hut, then the

whole system of the tribal chiefdom is damaged and the tribe eventually disintegrates.'

Recent marriages have further risked jeopardising the mystique of the institution by marrying outside the circle usually reserved for Royal Princes. Kate Middleton was middle class, Meghan Markle an American actress who was, furthermore, divorced. The national tribe embraced them, although sympathy has been strained by more recent actions of The Duke and Duchess of Sussex. Moments of awkwardness, such as during Prince Harry's wedding, when the bride's family was noticeably under-represented, were smoothed by senior members—and haven't many families, given the complications of modern family relationships, faced similar dilemmas at weddings? Amazingly, the Royal Family seems more in touch with popular sentiment than ever.

This would not have been possible without the blessing of the matriarch who headed that family: Elizabeth II. Families evolve and The Queen's ideas seemed to evolve in line with the experience of her children and grandchildren. 'For everything to stay the same, everything must change,' says Prince Tancredi in *The Leopard*. These are not words one could ever have expected to hear from the lips of The Queen, but as a wise guardian of the Windsors' destiny, she may have reached a similar conclusion. ✎

Above left: The whole family came together for Princess Eugenie's wedding in 2018. *Above right:* Having her mother for so much of her life was a geat comfort and support. *Left:* The Queen always enjoyed time with her grandchildren and great-grandchildren

The Royal Family appears on the balcony of Buckingham Palace to watch a flypast of 100 aircraft on July 10, 2018, to commemorate the centenary of the RAF

Keep calm and carry on

We'd all better get used to saying 'God Save The King' as The Queen's heirs will be male for at least three generations

WHEN she came to the throne, The Queen was not yet 26 and, like her father, felt unprepared for the role she was to take on. She will have taken consolation in knowing that her long reign meant that those who will follow her have had the opportunity to enjoy a life and gain experience before taking on the role.

In 2017, royal correspondent Robert Jobson profiled The Prince of Wales at 70 and described him as the 'Shadow King', the monarch in all but name as he took over many of his mother's duties, saying the change had come when she had asked him to lay her wreath at the Cenotaph.

At the same time, the younger members of the wider family also began to take on a greater role, preparing them—and the world—for the transition.

The Queen also met regularly with both Prince Charles and Prince William to pass on her extensive knowledge and insight.

As a result, she leaves a highly experienced King to ascend to the throne and a secure succession for many years to come, especially as the rules have been changed so that the crown will now pass to the first born, regardless of their gender. ✎

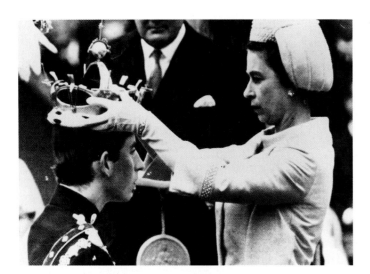

'As parents and grandparents, we feel great pride in seeing our family make their own unique contributions to society'

Christmas Message, 2008

Left: The investiture of The Prince of Wales in 1969. *Top:* The Queen and her heirs. *Above:* Over the past few years, Prince William has been learning the ins and outs of his future role from his grandmother

Top left: Prince George, pictured with his parents at Wembley Stadium for the England vs Germany match of the Euro 2020 championship, is already warming up to his role as a future king. *Above left:* 'You look familiar': Prince Harry's Sandhurst passing-out parade was a very proud occasion. *Above:* The Duke of Cambridge creates footballer Marcus Rashford an MBE at an investiture ceremony at Windsor Castle in 2021

Left: Having her family on engagements with her was always enjoyable. *Above:* Younger members of the family—such as The Duchess of Cambridge, joint-president of the Scouts —took on greater prominence in many roles in recent years

ℰⅡℛ

The family business

The name may have changed from Saxe-Coburg-Gotha to Windsor, but the dynasty continues to go from strength to strength

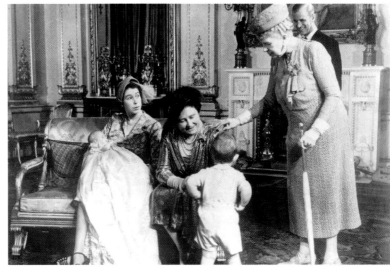

Mother Elizabeth II, grandmother Queen Elizabeth and great-grandmother Queen Mary try to corral Prince Charles at his sister's christening in 1950

Queen to Queen: from Victoria to Elizabeth (and beyond)

Victoria (1819–1901)
= Albert of Saxe-Coburg-Gotha (1819–61)

Edward VII (1841–1910)
= Alexandra of Denmark (1844–1925)

George V (1865–1936)
= Mary of Teck (1867–1953)

Edward VIII (Duke of Windsor) (1894–1972)
= Wallis Simpson (1896–1986)

George VI (1895–1952)
= Elizabeth Bowes-Lyon (1900–2002)

Elizabeth II (1926–2022)
= Philip Mountbatten, Duke of Edinburgh (1921–2021)

Charles (b. 1948)

= (1) Diana Spencer (1961–97)
= (2) Camilla Parker-Bowles (b. 1947)

William (b. 1982)
= Catherine Middleton (b. 1982)
George (b. 2013), Charlotte (b. 2015), Louis (b. 2018)

and

Henry (Harry) (b. 1984) = Meghan Markle (b. 1981)
Archie (b. 2019), Lilibet (b. 2021)

Anne (b. 1950)

= (1) Mark Phillips (b. 1948)
= (2) Timothy Laurence (b. 1955)

Peter (b. 1977)
= Autumn Kelly (b. 1978)
Savannah (b. 2010), Isla (b. 2012)

and

Zara (b. 1981)
= Michael Tindall (b. 1978)
Mia (b. 2014), Lena (b. 2018), Lucas (b. 2021)

Andrew (b. 1960)

= Sarah Ferguson (b. 1959)

Beatrice (b. 1988)
= Edoardo Mapelli Mozzi (b. 1983)
Sienna Mapelli Mozzi (b. 2021)

and

Eugenie (b. 1990)
= Jack Brooksbank (b. 1986)
August Brooksbank (b. 2021)

Edward (b. 1964)

= Sophie Rhys-Jones (b. 1965)

Louise (b. 2003)

and

James, Viscount Severn (b. 2007)

In *Anna Karenina*, Tolstoy wrote that 'happy families are all alike; every unhappy family is unhappy in its own way'. The Windsor dynasty has had a good deal of public sadness in its time, but, as for most families, its christenings have been happy occasions. Princess Elizabeth's (*above*) in 1926 was a more sedate affair than that of Prince Harry in 1984 (*top*), when a cheeky Prince William followed in his father's footsteps

The Imperial State Crown is set with 2,868 diamonds, 17 sapphires, 11 emeralds and hundreds of pearls. Weighing almost 2½lb, it was shortened by an inch for The Queen, who revealed to the BBC: 'You can't look down to read speeches at the State Opening of Parliament, because, if you did, your neck would break and it would fall off. There are some disadvantages to crowns, but, otherwise, they are quite important things.' The crown and state regalia travel to the State Opening of Parliament in their own carriage ahead of the monarch

Turning the pages of history

It is fitting that The Queen should have graced the Frontispiece of COUNTRY LIFE more than any other person. Here, we offer a collection of the photographs that reflect her remarkable life

Right: On the eve of her 21st birthday in 1947. On April 21, she broadcasted from Cape Town, vowing: 'I declare before you all that my whole life whether it be long or short shall be devoted to your service and the service of our great Imperial family to which we all belong'

Top: At Royal Lodge, Windsor, in 1946

Above: The Princess's first appearance on the COUNTRY LIFE Frontispiece, in May 1926

In July 1952, COUNTRY LIFE published the first formal portrait of the beautiful new Queen. The necklace she is wearing was originally composed of 21 diamonds that were presented to her in 1947 by the people of South Africa

A HAPPY GARDEN PORTRAIT AT ROYAL LODGE

"None love their country, but who love their home"

PRINCESS ELIZABETH and PRINCESS MARGARET ROSE

A photograph taken when the Princesses were watching the Punch and Judy show at Mr. Lancelot Hugh Smith's Hay Party at Mount Clare last week.

Above: In April 1937, the photogenic Royal Family was captured at Royal Lodge. The joyful image holds no trace of the stress George VI and Queen Elizabeth had been under due to the abdication crisis the previous winter

Right: Princess Elizabeth (*right*) and Princess Margaret are enthralled by a Punch and Judy show in 1935

H.R.H. PRINCESS ELIZABETH OF YORK

H.M. THE QUEEN AND H.R.H. PRINCESS ANNE

A new portrait, taken in the grounds of Buckingham Palace, of H.M. the Queen with Princess Anne, who last week celebrated her seventh birthday

HER MAJESTY THE QUEEN

A portrait taken on the small staircase in the Grand Entrance at Buckingham Palace. Her Majesty was due to arrive at Suva, Fiji Islands, to-day.

Starting to explore: the three-year-old Princess Elizabeth charmed the nation in July 1929

In 1957, The Queen was shown reading to Princess Anne, who had just celebrated her seventh birthday

After the Coronation, The Queen, here depicted in December 1953, embarked on a long overseas tour ➤

COUNTRY LIFE

Vol. XCI. No. 2350   JANUARY 30, 1942

Studio Lisa

THE PRINCESSES IN PANTOMIME

The Princess Elizabeth and Princess Margaret as Florizel and Cinderella in the Christmas pantomime that they produced to raise funds for the Royal Households Concerts Wool Fund. The cast included officers' daughters, evacuees from London and village children.

COUNTRY LIFE

Vol. LXXXV.—No. 2207   SATURDAY, MAY 6th, 1939

AT BUCKINGHAM PALACE
A recent photograph of Their Majesties the King and Queen with their daughters

Above: **A 1939 family picture taken at Buckingham Palace. On May 17, George VI and Queen Elizabeth began a tour of Canada, the US and Newfoundland**

Left: **Fairy-tale princesses: Elizabeth (*left*) and Margaret performing as Florizel and Cinderella in January, 1942. Their pantomime raised significant funds for charity**

COUNTRY LIFE

Vol. CXXII No. 3171   OCTOBER 24, 1957

H.M. THE QUEEN
A portrait of H.M. the Queen taken on the eve of her State visit to Canada and the United States of America

Above: **In October 1957, The Queen wore the regal circlet of George IV, who wore it to his Coronation over a large plumed hat—it hadn't been worn by a king since then**

Far left: **Helping out with the harvest at Sandringham, September 1943**

Left: **With the four-year-old Princess Anne (wearing her mother's first pearl necklace) and the seven-year-old Prince Charles in 1955**

COUNTRY LIFE

Vol. XCIV. No. 2433   SEPTEMBER 3, 1943

HARVEST-TIME AT SANDRINGHAM
H.R.H. Princess Elizabeth leads one of the horses in the Norfolk harvest-fields

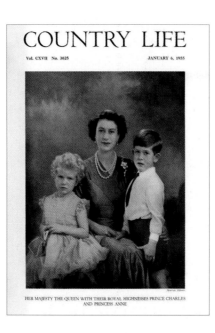

COUNTRY LIFE

Vol. CXVII No. 3025   JANUARY 6, 1955

HER MAJESTY THE QUEEN WITH THEIR ROYAL HIGHNESSES PRINCE CHARLES
AND PRINCESS ANNE

The proud mother poses with the infant Prince Charles, swathed in silk and Honiton lace, after his christening on December 15, 1948

Sultan, a fine bay Thoroughbred, was presented to The Queen by the President of Pakistan. The keen horsewoman is pictured on him two years later, in 1961

In 1945, Princess Elizabeth joined the Women's Auxiliary Territorial Service as No 230873 Second Subaltern Elizabeth Windsor. Here, she poses proudly in her uniform for the Frontis-piece in July that year

Above: The 14-year-old Princess Elizabeth and Queen Elizabeth pictured in February, 1941. Such portraits boosted wartime morale

Right: Some 50,000 people massed outside Parliament House in Wellington, New Zealand, when The Queen visited in May 1954. Three in every four New Zealanders managed to see her as she visited 46 towns and cities ⬎

The mother of our family of nations

A tireless traveller and ambassador, The Queen shaped Britain's international relationships and the politics of the globe as much as any politician

Written by Jane Watkins

Facing page: A true New York tickertape welcome in 1957. *Left:* Laughter in Nigeria in 2003, The Queen's first visit to the country since it gained its independence in 1956

VETERAN royal correspondent Robert Hardman succinctly summed up The Queen's world-wide influence during her long reign and how her particular brand of 'soft diplomacy' proved key by writing: 'Few things better illustrate the scale of change during this reign than the fact that most of the nations on earth have only come into existence since the Queen came to the throne. Yet she has visited most of them.'

When The Queen was born, Britain was still suffering the after-effects of the First World War and, on her accession, we were rebuilding after the Second. Since then, countries and regimes have come and gone and our Empire has become the Common-wealth, but the latter organisation, which she holds close to her heart, has not only survived, but thrived. Notably, it has done so in a manner that should have offered

a salutary lesson to the European Union and the way Brexit was handled.

From the start, the new organisation was to be based on mutual assistance and The Queen had no intention of being an Empress by another name, merely a guiding hand: 'The Commonwealth bears no resemblance to the empires of the past. It is an entirely new conception built on the highest qualities of the spirit of man: friendship, loyalty, and the desire for freedom and peace.'

In her Christmas Message of 1991, she made clear its continuing value: 'At the Commonwealth Heads of Government Meeting in Zimbabwe this autumn, we saw an example of mutual tolerance and respect for the views of others on an international scale. Leaders of the 50 nations came together to discuss the future. They met in peace, they talked freely, they listened, they found much on which to agree and they

set a new direction for the Commonwealth. I am sure that each derived strength and reassurance in the process.'

It is no underestimate to say that the decades during which The Queen presided over the Commonwealth have been the most tumultuous in our history. Society saw swift and remarkable changes, technology revo-lutionised the way in which we live and the world population rose from about 2.5 billion to 7.8 billion. The Commonwealth alone is currently home to about 2.4 billion citizens.

Like the calm eye in the heart of a tornado, The Queen was a remarkable constant, a symbol to which many people felt an instinctive attachment, and she skilfully managed to stay above the political fray, although always employing her consider-able experience to offer sympathy and insightful comments. 'She can talk intelli-gently about politics and economics ➤

of all the countries,' remarked Bob Hawke, Australia's former prime minister.

She was the most famous woman in the world, but the most unknowable, yet her subjects around the globe viewed her with affection. Sir John Major captured this feeling best: 'She is the most widely travelled head of state in history; indeed, around the world, whenever anyone refers to "The Queen", they mean "Our Queen".'

The Commonwealth first came into being, through the Balfour Declaration at the Imperial Conference, in 1926, the same year that The Queen was born, and was formally constituted by the London Declaration of 1949, in which it was stated that members were to be 'equal in status'.

In 2009, she recognised her personal link to the organisation: 'I have been closely associated with the Commonwealth through most of its existence. The personal and living bond I have enjoyed with leaders, and with people the world over, has always been more important in promoting our unity than symbolism alone. The Commonwealth is not an organisation with a mission. It is, rather, an opportunity for its people to work together to achieve practical solutions to problems.'

Those issues are not simply political, either. The Commonwealth offers a number of ways in which its nations can find common ground. The 2009 Christmas Message made this clear: 'In many aspects of our lives, whether in sport, the environment, business or culture, the Commonwealth connection remains vivid and enriching. It is, in lots of ways, the face of the future. And with continuing support and dedication, I am confident that this diverse Commonwealth of nations can strengthen the common bond that transcends politics, religion, race and economic circumstances.'

'It is an association which starts with a prejudice in favour of friendship'

Sir Alec Douglas-Home

That Her Majesty's first moments as Queen famously came when she was up a tree in Kenya is a potent symbol of how integral her relationship with her overseas territories was from the first and her accession felt like a new beginning. On April 18, 1955, Sir Winston Churchill stated, with extraordinary prescience: 'I felt the impact of a new

personality upon our unfolding history... I regard it as the most direct mark of God's favour that the whole structure of our new-formed Commonwealth has been illuminated by a sparkling presence at its summit.'

From the start of her reign, Commonwealth trips were a colourful feature—indeed, her first tour as Queen, in 1953–54, took her 43,618 miles over six months to Canada, Bermuda, Jamaica, Panama, Fiji, Tonga, New Zealand, Australia, the Cocos Islands, Ceylon, Aden, Uganda, Libya, Malta and Gibraltar. A staggering 75% of the Australian population came out to see her.

'I set out on this journey in order to see as much as possible of the people and countries of the Commonwealth and Empire,' she said. 'I want to show that the Crown is not merely an abstract symbol of our unity but a personal and living bond between you and me.'

Elizabeth II was the first British monarch to circumnavigate the globe and her first tour was the longest single journey made by any of our rulers

The advent of air travel meant that visits could occur more frequently and require

unique,' The Princess Royal said in *The Queen: Her Commonwealth Story* in 2018. 'She's been in that position of being an honorary man for a long time. People get used to the fact you can have a conversation about things you wouldn't normally talk to women about.'

The Queen's invention of the walkabout in 1972 was a masterstroke and an indication of how well she knew what was required of a changing monarchy. 'It really was ground-breaking territory,' recalled her former private secretary Sir William Heseltine. 'It made an entirely new relationship between The Queen and the public.'

And no mere politician could have achieved, through a simple visit, the change brought about by her trip to Ireland in 2011, the first by a British monarch for more than a century, capped by her charmingly beginning a speech with a few words in the native tongue.

'There is no doubt that The Queen provides the magnet'

Boris Johnson

That same visit provides a wonderful example of Her Majesty using something in her arsenal that no male monarch could pull off: an emotional appeal through what she wore. Arriving in Ireland, she stepped off the plane in emerald green and, later, there was a white dress adorned with 2,091 hand-sewn silk shamrocks finished off with a crystal Irish-harp brooch that had been created specially for the state dinner.

It is well known that Her Majesty has particularly enjoyed her visits to Africa, where crowds have met her with an exuberance unequalled at most international events. The feeling is returned: 'Africa has a unique place in my affections and there is always something so very special about the warmth and enthusiasm of the traditional African welcome.'

Of the Commonwealth member states, The Queen remained as monarch of 16, which are known as the Commonwealth realms and include Canada, Australia, Papua New Guinea, New Zealand and Jamaica, as well as the UK. Of the rest, 32 are republics and five have different monarchs.

The Commonwealth has remained one of the most successful international institutions. It is striking that countries such as Cameroon, Mozambique and Rwanda, ➤

less time away from Britain. Although she was never a fan of flying, despite making the equivalent of 42 turns around the globe (1,032,513 miles), she did enjoy meeting the people. Charles Anson, The Queen's press secretary in the 1990s, explained to the *Radio Times*: 'I always felt that the Queen enjoys travel. She is genuinely curious about people, their different cultures, traditions and quirks.'

The Empire was said to cover a quarter of the earth's surface and, over the course of her reign, it's hard to think of a part she did not visit. She went to all the countries of the Commonwealth, except Cameroon and Rwanda, which joined after she had begun to scale down her overseas travel. Two of the most important countries she never visited were Greece and Israel, the latter due to security concerns and the former due to the country's treatment of the Duke of Edinburgh and his family when

he was a child. She has also never been to Madagascar, Cuba or Peru.

It is undeniable that part of the success of these trips is due to the quiet charisma of The Queen. Although her upbringing and background are redolent of an earlier age of restraint, modesty and self-effacement, there is a sure-footedness to her public appearances, particularly when abroad, that would be the envy of even the most adept politician.

In the television documentary *Queen of the World*, Baroness Scotland, the current Commonwealth Secretary-General described how startling her influence really was: 'She was a young woman leader at a time in history when there weren't any young women leading. Her skill was so profound that many people forgot that she was a young woman—she was just "The Queen".'

'Her length of time in that position and her ability to talk to those leaders is virtually

In 1986, The Queen achieved a long-held wish
to visit China, where *Yilishabai Nuwang*,
as she was called, and her consort *Feilipu
Qinwang* were rapturously received. It was
only her second state visit to a Communist
country, the first being to Yugoslavia in 1972.
As part of the tour, the couple visited the
terracotta warriors of Xian, which had only
been rediscovered in 1974

which were never part of the Empire, have been able to join and countries as diverse as Sudan, Yemen and Algeria have all applied to join.

It is a measure of how much The Queen's contribution was valued that her 'sincere wish' for the future of the Commonwealth was granted. In April 2018, the Commonwealth leaders unanimously agreed that The Prince of Wales should take on his mother's non-hereditary role as honorary head of the organisation on her death. The Prince stated: 'For my part, the Commonwealth has been a fundamental feature of my life for as long as I can remember, beginning with my first visit to Malta when I was just five years old.' Since then, he had visited another 43 of the 53 nations.

'She has been the rock that has kept this organisation sturdy and true to its positive belief'

Nana Dankwa Akufo-Addo,
President of the Republic of Ghana

In 2018, The Duchess of Sussex surprised her husband by including the flowers of all the Commonwealth countries on her wedding veil, echoing The Queen's Coronation dress, although The Duke and Duchess of Sussex no longer serve as president and vice-president of The Queen's Commonwealth Trust. Nonetheless, the trust is still operating as a powerful force for good, advising and supporting millions of young people seeking to transform their homes, in fields ranging from agriculture to healthcare.

Announcing the decision to follow The Queen's wishes, British Prime Minister Theresa May said that the Commonwealth itself existed in 'no small measure because of the vision, duty and steadfast service of Her Majesty in nurturing the growth of this remarkable family of nations'.

The vitally important work the organisation does can be summed up in The Queen's own words from the 1993 Christmas message: 'We, the peoples of the 50 nations of the Commonwealth—more than a quarter of the world's population—have, as members of one of the largest families, a great responsibility. By working together, we can help the rest of the world become a more humane and happier place.' ➹

Seen close up, the exquisite detail that goes into any garment worn by The Queen—as well as her tiny proportions—is evident in this turquoise-silk dress with silver floral embroidery by Hardy Amies and a pale-blue and gold evening dress by Normal Hartnell, on show in the Royal Collection's 'Fashioning a Reign' exhibition in 2016

Clothes maketh the monarch

Hailed by *Vogue* in 2007 as one of the most glamorous women in the world, Elizabeth II stood out from the crowd for all the right reasons. Let's take a peek inside her wardrobe

Written by Matthew Dennison

THE Queen's clothes, royal dress-maker Norman Hartnell wrote, required 'a non-sensational elegance'. He was well placed to judge. He first dressed The Queen when, as the nine-year-old Princess Elizabeth of York, she was one of eight bridesmaids at the wedding of her uncle, Prince Henry, Duke of Gloucester. He would continue to provide clothes for his best-known client for more than four decades, including her wedding dress and Coronation gown.

If, for much of her reign, Elizabeth II was criticised for her choice of clothes, even being accused of dowdiness, it was Hartnell, who, in the 1950s, was largely responsible for transforming the young Queen into the woman that Prince Philip described as the world's 'sweetheart'.

Hartnell had first designed clothes for The Queen's mother, Queen Elizabeth, including heavily embroidered evening dresses with crinoline skirts, inspired by portraits by Winterhalter. For the 20-something Elizabeth II, he evolved a style inspired by Dior's 'New Look': a mix of sharp tailoring, tiny waists and big skirts.

In combination with The Queen's flawless complexion, lightbulb smile and magnificent jewellery, it served to invest a young ➤

Left: The two most photographed women in the world in 1961: when the Kennedys visited London. According to Cecil Beaton, the First Lady 'was unimpressed by the palace furnishings and by The Queen's dress and hairstyle'.
Below left: White lace to beat the Australian heat and emphasise her tiny waist in February 1954. The aqua parasol added a zing of colour.
Below right: Early Hartnell outfits, such as this example from a Paris visit in 1948, were inspired by Dior's 'New Look'

'Her real charm, like her mother's,
does not carry across in her
photographs, and each time one
sees her, one is delighted how much
more serene, magnetic, and, at the
same time, meltingly sympathetic,
she is than one had imagined.
In the photographs, there is a certain
heaviness which is not there in
real life, and one misses... the effect
of the dazzlingly fresh complexion,
the clear regard from the glass-blue
eyes, and the gentle, all-pervading
sweetness of her smile'

Cecil Beaton

Regal radiance: on state visits abroad, The Queen was renowned for dressing to respect her hosts and for adding a local touch to her outfits. Here, she is in New Delhi, India, and her Norman Hartnell-designed dress is made up of lotus flowers—India's national flower—embellished with pearls, sequins and bugle beads. It is worn with Queen Alexandra's Kokoshnik tiara woman of conservative tastes, lacking personal vanity, with a film-star glamour that, during her first decade on the throne, wowed style pundits across the globe.

Throughout the 1950s, Hartnell and fellow British dressmaker Hardy Amies provided the new Queen with a wardrobe carefully calculated to underline her unique status, a look that was opulent, but regal. Both men designed glittering, lavishly embroidered evening gowns in sumptuous fabrics.

The full-length, one-shouldered gold lamé and lace dress that was worn by the Queen in Wellington, New Zealand, in 1954 and a diaphanous, glittering dress of white tulle embroidered in shell patterns in gold, silver and diamanté made for the Portuguese state visit of 1957 were high-octane show-stoppers, but when The Queen was due to meet real film stars, including Marilyn Monroe, at the Royal Film Performance of 1956, Hartnell persuaded her to wear a simple, full-skirted black velvet dress that, partnered with diamonds and emeralds, successfully eclipsed showier choices.

> ## 'We discuss clothes, make-up, jewellery. We say: "Would this piece of jewellery look nice with that outfit?"'
>
> Angela Kelly

The Queen's dressers and her couturiers agreed that she considered her wardrobe as an aspect of the public face of monarchy; otherwise, she didn't lavish particular thought on something that didn't interest her greatly. Dressmakers throughout the reign were not invited to offer advice, although The Queen herself had a gimlet eye for detail. In 1990, for example, she returned a John Anderson design for a knee-length red-wool coat annotated with the comment 'Neckline of coat and reverse a bit low and long for me'. The design was amended accordingly.

Her wardrobe was not conditioned by personal preferences, but what The Queen understood as the requirements of the job. Her trademark look of loose coats with matching dresses evolved in the 1960s and remained largely unchanged until her death, adapted by later dressmakers Stuart Parvin and Angela Kelly.

It was partly the creation of Hartnell and arose amid preparations for The Queen's

Above: Stuart Parvin created this dress and coat for Prince Harry's wedding and Angela Kelly made the hat. *Facing page:* The Queen wearing the Girls of Great Britain and Ireland tiara, given to her as a wedding present by Queen Mary, and the Crown Rubies parure

state visit to India in 1961: a look that was appropriately formal for a working monarch, but also manageable in high temperatures. The tour saw some of her most successful 'working' clothes: a lavender dress with voluminous matching duster coat worn in New Delhi; an opalescent pearl-grey heavy-silk dress and matching coat.

Later in her reign, The Queen invariably teamed coats in a single, striking colour with printed frocks that picked up the dominant colour note.

She dressed to be seen. Both Queen Mary and Queen Elizabeth had worn pastel colours, a convention largely followed by Elizabeth II in the first years of her reign. Her fondness for pastel blue led to a degree of ribaldry on the satirical television programme

That Was The Week That Was. Later, she embraced a greater spectrum of colours, including vibrant shades guaranteed to make her stand out in the largest crowd, saying: 'I have to be seen to be believed.'

The vivid-green outfit she wore for Trooping the Colour on her official birthday in 2016 caused a sensation on social media, spawning the hashtag 'Neon@90'. Only in the designs commissioned for evening and state dresses did The Queen stick to a palette restricted to white, gold and silver.

It was a mark of her success that most of her subjects failed to take much notice of many of her clothes. Instead, they recognised, at a glance, her distinctive daytime look of coat and dress, matching hat, matching gloves, shoes and handbag, three-row ➤

Above: One thing The Queen always wears is her engagement ring, which was designed by Prince Philip and made from diamonds belonging to a tiara of his mother's. *Right and far right:* Sketches for The Queen's wedding dress and an outfit from 1995

pearl necklace and brooch or, in the evening, long dress, large necklace, tiara, gloves and family orders. It was as much a uniform as that of any Starbucks barista and, in the same way, it said more about the job than the woman herself.

Those with an eagle eye for detail could have pinpointed favourite brooches or hats she wore more than once: overwhelmingly, her clothing choices reinforced the suggestion of dignified kindliness and necessary formality that characterised her approach to sovereignty. The Queen was reported to love best jewels with historic associations: George IV's diamond diadem, which she wore every year on arrival at the State Opening of Parliament, and Queen Victoria's Jubilee necklace of diamonds and large pearls. As much as anything she said, her wardrobe choices reiterated the idea of continuity that was central to her concept of constitutional monarchy in modern times.

Above all, after the early years, it was a style determined by practical choices: shoes sufficiently comfortable for long hours standing and walking, hats that could be guaranteed not to blow away and skirts that remained in place, with no untoward glimpses of royal flesh. Maureen Rose, whose designs for the Queen in the 1990s included flowing chiffon evening dresses, explained her own approach: 'I always put in a straight lining, fitted to the body, so that even if the dress blew up, the lining wouldn't.'

Norman Hartnell.

A certain style

The handbag

Her Majesty preferred Launer bags and owned more than 200—her preferred styles were the Royale and the black-patent Traviata. They all had a long handle to ease the process of handshaking. She also used her handbag to signal to her ladies in waiting. If she wanted to leave an event within five minutes, she would place it on the table. To wrap up a dull conversation, she either placed the bag on the floor or switched it from one arm to another, prompting staff to rescue her (she also rotated her rings to convey the same message). 'It would be very worrying if you were talking to The Queen and saw the handbag move from one hand to the other,' warned royal historian Hugo Vickers. What was in the bag? A mirror, Clarins lipstick, reading glasses, a mint lozenge, a fountain pen, a crisp £5 note for church collections and a portable hook to hang the bag from a table. It was also believed to hold good-luck charms given to her by her children, including miniature dogs, horses and saddles, as well as family photographs

The shoes

Although The Queen was only 5ft 3in, she didn't compensate by wearing high heels, sticking to a practical heel height of 2¼in or lower if cobbles or uneven terrain were to be tackled. Anello and Davide handmade her shoes for decades. The company's David Hyatt said: 'We supply one or two pairs a year and occasionally renew the tops and re-heel them. The Queen doesn't waste money. She's no Imelda Marcos.' For extra comfort, each of her black-patent 'work shoes' contained an extra insole and a member of the Buckingham Palace staff would wear the shoes in for Her Majesty to ensure they didn't rub. Stuart Parvin, who dressed her for many years, explained: 'The Queen can never say "I'm uncomfortable, I can't walk any more"'

Gloves, scarves, umbrellas and handkerchiefs

The Queen's preferred length of glove was 6in—from 1947, her pairs were provided by Cornelia James. Her Majesty had an extensive collection of Hermès silk squares and Fulton made her a clear umbrella with a trim to match every outfit. Handkerchiefs were plain white with a royal motif for daytime events, but a tartan one came out in the country

Make-up

The Queen was always seen with a neutral shade of nail polish—in fact, she wore Essie's Ballet Slippers. The British brand was launched in 1981 and she became a devoted fan a year later. Clarins and Floris held Royal Warrants for skincare, make-up and fragrance, although she also favoured Elizabeth Arden lipsticks

The hats

Never wide-brimmed so as not to obscure The Queen's face, they were also not too tall, which would make getting out of a car difficult. The back should

Matching coat in blue linen mixture lined in Abraham printed silk of the dress.

HARDY AMIES

not have an impact on the collar. If a hat was a key part of the outfit, a scarf to match was created in case the hat got wet or was damaged. From 2006, Rachel Trevor-Morgan was a favourite milliner

The clothes

The Queen favoured slim, three-quarter-length sleeves to ensure they didn't trail in soup. She never took off her coat in public and the hems of her dresses fell beneath the knee and were weighted. Elizabeth II was only photographed wearing trousers at a public engagement once—during the tour of Canada in 1970, young dressmaker Ian Thomas made her a matte-silk trouser suit in a bid to modernise her look. Designers had to choose fabrics that would not crease if Her Majesty had to travel by car or sit for extended periods—they also had to fall appropriately as she stepped from a vehicle. For evening dresses, heavy beading could be uncomfortable and too much fabric was cumbersome—splits and pleats were built in to make it easier to tackle stairs gracefully

Dressing The Queen

For big occasions, up to 12 people staffed her wardrobe department, including Angela Kelly, a personal assistant, plus three dressmakers, a milliner and four dressers. Designers gave names to The Queen's outfits and dressers kept handwritten wardrobe diaries; for example, if Her Majesty wore red on a visit to the south of England, that colour would be avoided for several months, even if the designs were totally different. On the day of an event, a team of three designers prepared the outfit, as well as a choice of accompanying brooches, shoes, gloves and headscarves ↰

Pomp and circumstance

A sense of duty was one of the hallmarks of Elizabeth II's reign, whether it was at events of national celebration or of personal importance

Written by Jane Watkins

'I THOUGHT it all very, very wonderful and I expect the Abbey did, too. The arches and beams at the top were covered with a sort of haze of wonder as Papa was crowned,' a dazzled 11-year-old Princess Elizabeth wrote of her father's Coronation in 1937.

For the many decades of her reign, no one outside her inner circle knew whether the great pageantry of monarchy continued to delight The Queen, although a close friend claimed that the Sovereign always believed 'implicitly in the ceremonial'.

The structure of each year was underpinned by public spectacles, many of ancient origin, which demonstrate the historic grandeur of the Crown and its place in our constitution and national life: the Royal Maundy Service (Easter), Trooping the Colour and the Garter Service (June), the autumn State Opening of Parliament, which Her Majesty first attended in 1947, and the Remembrance Day poppy-laying ceremony at the Cenotaph in November.

Not all events are grand, however. Young and old members of the public clearly felt the emotional outpouring of being able to see or meet the Sovereign at visits, walkabouts or Crathie church at Christmas, surrounded by her family. The crowds filling the Mall on big occasions, making the famous road a sea of red, white and blue, expressed a national outpouring of affection and respect.

Trooping the Colour

The Queen attended every Trooping the Colour, except for 1955, when the event was cancelled due to a national train strike. Until 1987, she inspected her troops on horseback—most notably on Burmese. Not even having six blank shots fired at them in 1981 unsettled the dignified pair.

Remembrance Day

Until 2017, when she asked The Prince of Wales to take over for her permanently, The Queen laid her wreath at the Cenotaph on Remembrance Sunday every year of her reign, except in 1959, 1961, 1963, 1968, 1983 and 1999, when she was either pregnant or overseas on official visits.   ➤

State Opening of Parliament

Elizabeth II opened Parliament every year as monarch, except in 1959 and 1963, when she was pregnant. The Queen's Speech was not drafted by her, but by the Government, and outlined its plans and legislation for the coming year. The speech was carried by the Lord Chancellor in a silk bag and presented to Her Majesty on bended knee. Both Houses gathered in the Lords to hear it.

Supporting business

Thanks to modern travel, Elizabeth II has been able to visit more parts of her realms than any other monarch before her, visiting and promoting British businesses. Her profile is key for the UK's £160 billion annual exports: when Chinese consumers were asked what words they associated with Britain, she topped the list, with 25.1%.

Garden parties

More than 1.5 million people have attended garden parties at Buckingham Palace or the Palace of Holyroodhouse. About 30,000 people attend the three summer events at Buckingham Palace and one party at Holyroodhouse, consuming some 27,000 cups of tea, 20,000 sandwiches and 20,000 slices of cake on each occasion. The people who are invited have all made a positive impact on their communities in some way.

Additional garden parties can be held—for example, there was one to celebrate the 50th anniversary of The Duke of Edinburgh's Award Scheme in 2006 and the Territorial Army's 100th anniversary in 2008. For The Queen's 80th birthday in 2006, the gardens were transformed into scenes from children's books for the Children's Party at the Palace. In 2015, the centenaries of the WI and Blind Veterans UK were celebrated. ➤

Orders of Chivalry

Inspired by the legends of King Arthur, Edward II created his own group of honourable knights and bestowed upon them the Order of the Garter. This is now the most senior order of chivalry in Britain. It comprises the Sovereign, several senior members of the Royal Family and 24 knights who have been chosen in recognition of their service to national life or to the sovereign personally. In June each year, the knights and officers of the order walk in procession to St George's Chapel in velvet cloaks and plumed hats, in one of the most picturesque spectacles in the royal calendar.

North of the border, the Order of the Thistle was revived by James II and is Scotland's highest honour. The order is celebrated in a service each July at St Giles's Cathedral, Edinburgh.

'I often draw strength from meeting ordinary people doing extraordinary things'

Christmas message, 2016

Maundy Money

On Maundy Thursday, the day before Good Friday, the Sovereign distributes silver coins, or Maundy Money, as symbolic alms to the elderly. The service is held at a different church each year (The Queen stipulated it could not be held in London more than once a decade) and recipients are nominated by their diocese. One man and one woman are chosen for each year of the Monarch's life (including the current year). To celebrate the Diamond Jubilee in 2012, recipients were selected from all 44 dioceses in the UK.

Viewing it as an extremely important part of her devotional life, Her Majesty was only unable to attend the service four times, until it was interrupted by the pandemic.

Each recipient is given two leather purses, supplied by Barrow Hepburn & Gale: a white one holding coins to the value of the Monarch's age and a red one holding a £5 and a 50p coin. Each year, there are fewer than 2,000 complete sets.

Getty; Shutterstock

Walkabouts

Her Majesty continued to fulfill a packed diary of events right up to her death—for example, in 2017, she still undertook an amazing 292 engagements—although in latter years, some of her accustomed duties were distributed to other members of the family. Although she ceased to travel overseas in 2015, she continued to meet her British

subjects. The last country she visited was Malta, a country dear to her heart, as she had begun her married life there.

On the 1970 tour of Australia and New Zealand, The Queen decided that she wanted to meet a wider range of people than officials and dignitaries and a new tradition, the walkabout, was born.

In the documentary *The Queen at 90*, the Countess of Wessex explained: '[The Queen] needs to stand out for people to be able to say "I saw the queen". Don't forget that, when she turns up somewhere, the crowds are two, three, four, 10, 15 deep and someone wants to be able to say they saw a bit of The Queen's hat as she went past.'

Investitures

In 1992, The Queen stated that she considered investitures to be the most important of her public ceremonies. Annually, some 3,000 people receive awards in about 25 ceremonies. These are redolent with tradition—the sword used to dub new knights belonged to George VI and the Monarch enters the room attended by two Gurkha orderly officers, in a tradition that was begun by Queen Victoria in 1876.

Christmas message

From 1952, The Queen broadcast a Christmas message every year, except 1969, when the documentary *Royal Family* was shown and a written message was sent. She made her first radio address when she was only 14.

From 1957, the message was televised: 'Twenty-five years ago, my grandfather broadcast the first of these Christmas messages. Today is another landmark, because television has made it possible for many of you to see me in your homes on Christmas Day. My own family often gather round to watch television, as they are this moment, and that is how I imagine you now.'

The Christmas message was initally shown live, but, from 1960, it was recorded in advance so that tapes can be sent to the Commonwealth countries, so that they can show it at a more convenient time for local audiences. In 2012, it was broadcast in 3D. Admiring television crews gave Elizabeth II the nickname One-Take Windsor for her polished delivery.

Audiences

Each week, usually on Wednesday evenings, The Queen met with the current Prime Minister—Boris Johnson became the 14th in 2019—to discuss Government matters. Before each Budget, she also met with the Chancellor of the Exchequer.

Sir John Major explained the value of Her Majesty's counsel to Sky News: 'The Queen, of course, has been seeing State papers since 1952. There is no one anywhere in the world who has seen and read and absorbed so many State papers as our Queen.'

The meetings are entirely private and the conversations kept in strict confidence.

She also held audiences with officials from other countries and every newly appointed ambassador or Commonwealth high commissioner proceeded to the palace to present their Letters of Credence or Letters of High Commission. ➤

Animal magic

Away from the glamour and ceremonial, The Queen liked nothing better than to get out into the fresh air with her horses and dogs. Along the way, she became one of the most successful racehorse owners and made the corgi popular

Written by Kate Green and Paula Lester

As at home in the saddle as on the throne

THINK of the fabric of any year in The Queen's life and it would be hard to not include images of her at the centre of the equestrian world, whether happily waving to a cheering crowd at Royal Ascot, inspecting the showing lines at Royal Windsor or simply hacking out in Windsor Great Park—most recently with sons Prince Andrew and Prince Edward, as well as with the latter's children, Lady Louise Windsor and James, Viscount Severn.

Even on an official visit, horses get special attention. At trainer Paul Nicholls's stables in March 2019, her joy was evident at being able to feed carrots to some of his equally contented charges. And on a day of equine engagements later that month, she nearly lost her handbag when a police horse named Windsor grew jealous of her generosity to one of his fellow mounts. ➤

Facing page: Admiring the gleam of a perfect turn out: visiting the King's Troop in 2017.
Above: The Queen inherited her lifelong love of horses from her father, George VI

Above: The Queen's pleasure at winning the Gold Cup in 2012 with Estimate is evident. *Facing page:* Coming sixth at Ascot in 1961, in the traditional morning race on the last day

'The new police horse isn't used to all the cheers so I had to give him an extra Polo,' she explained with great insight.

Elizabeth II has lent a gravitas and expertise to the British equestrian scene that are the envy of the rest of the world. They represent the continuance of a royal tradition that was established with the founding of the Royal Stud at Hampton Court in the 16th century and continued with Charles II moving his Court to Newmarket every year and Queen Anne spotting the potential for a racecourse at Ascot.

Early photographs show Princess Elizabeth sitting confidently on a black Shetland pony, Peggy, a fourth-birthday present, and she and Princess Margaret were sent to learn to ride and drive with Horace Smith and his daughter Sybil in Maidenhead.

In her later years, Her Majesty rode less and described herself as 'rather a fair-weather rider now. I don't like getting cold and wet'. Even so, she will have gained contentment from knowing that her love of riding had been passed on through the generations—in 2018, great-grandchildren Prince George and Princess Charlotte began lessons with her eldest granddaughter, Zara Tindall, who followed in the footsteps of her mother, The Princess Royal, to become an international medal-winning rider.

'She has an ability to get horses psychologically attuned to what she wants and then persuade them to enjoy it'

Sir John Miller, Crown Equerry

In 1945, Princess Elizabeth and her sister won the private turnout (driving) class at Royal Windsor Horse Show with their pony Hans. The show remains an annual diary date and was the scene of The Queen's 90th-birthday celebrations, with horses flown in from all over the world for a spectacular pageant against the scenic backdrop of a floodlit Windsor Castle.

The Queen's father, grandfather and great-grandfather all owned racehorses: Edward VII was the last monarch to have a Derby winner (his home-bred Persimmon in 1896) and his horses were trained at Kingsclere in Hampshire, where Her Majesty had some of her 25 or so racehorses in training with Andrew Balding.

The Queen inherited George VI's Flat racehorses (her mother had the jumpers) and this got off to a thrilling and, no doubt, pleasantly distracting start when Aureole finished second in the Derby only days after the Coronation.

The distinctive royal racing colours—purple, gold and red with a black-velvet hat with gold fringe—have been carried to victory on her behalf more than 800 times and she was leading owner in the 1950s, before the might of Middle Eastern-owned horsepower began to dominate. However, the Derby was the only Classic The Queen never managed to win. ➤

Magnificent monarch: The Queen mounted on Burmese at Trooping the Colour in 1972. Her Majesty rode the horse, a gift from the Royal Canadian Mounted Police at the event for 18 consecutive years, between 1969 and 1986. Black armbands are being worn to mark the recent death of the Duke of Windsor

In 2013, The Queen was named Racehorse Owner of the Year for her contribution to the sport and in recognition of her first Ascot Gold Cup winner, Estimate, trained by Sir Michael Stoute. In Diamond Jubilee year, it was her first Grade One winner since Dunfermline, winner of the Epsom Oaks in 1977—Silver Jubilee year—and pictures of a delighted monarch were beamed around the world.

The Queen set aside diary time every year to visit her horses in training and was hugely knowledgeable about bloodlines. She stood two stallions at the Royal Stud at Sandringham—Royal Applause and the Derby winner Motivator—which had been bought by The Queen's racing manager, John Warren.

'It could have been disastrous, but she quietly reassured her mount and all was well'

The moment blank shots were fired during the 1981 Trooping the Colour

Her Majesty was an elegant, competent horsewoman, as was demonstrated in a terrifying moment during Trooping the Colour in 1981, when blank shots were fired from the crowd. The result could have been disastrous, but The Queen quietly reassured her mount, Burmese, and all was well. Burmese was a much-loved sight; a gift in 1969 from Royal Canadian Mounted Police, the horse carried The Queen a remarkable 18 times for Trooping the Colour.

The Queen had followed eventing ever since Badminton Horse Trials was started by the 10th Duke of Beaufort in 1949; her annual visit would include hacking out with the Duke and Princess Margaret and watching the cross-country from a rug beside the lake with the rest of the crowd.

In 1974, she presented the trophy to her then son-in-law, Capt Mark Phillips, after his victory on her horse Columbus, a mount that was deemed to be too strong for The Princess Royal. Another happy day was the 1971 European Championships at Burghley, when she was able to present the gold medal to her daughter, winner of the individual title on Doublet, bred by The Queen out of a polo pony.

The Queen also owned Countryman III, second at Badminton with the 11th Duke of Beaufort, David Somerset, and ridden by Bertie Hill at the 1956 Olympic Games in Stockholm. The cross-country course

'My corgis are family,' The Queen (shown here in 1936 with Dookie, her first corgi, and his mate, Jane, parents of Carol and Crackers) once said and the connection was immediate

there was fearsome and became slippery after overnight rain; Countryman became straddled over a fence that collapsed, but, nonetheless, completed the course and helped Britain to win a first Olympic team gold medal in eventing.

It was the Duke of Edinburgh who said that horses were 'great levellers' and The Queen always took the vicissitudes of ownership with equanimity, delighted by her own success, but equally pleased for others. Her tangible pleasure, in turn, gave great pleasure to everyone else. *KG*

Canine companions

HAVING been given her first dog —a Cairn terrier—at the age of three by her uncle, the Prince of Wales, the young Princess Elizabeth quickly developed a natural affection for animals.

This rapport was further bolstered in 1933, when her father introduced her first corgi, Dookie, into the Royal Household. When mated with a bitch called Jane, Dookie fathered two puppies born one ➤

'Her Majesty closely follows their
development. If The Queen wasn't
The Queen, she would have made
a wonderful trainer. She has such an
affinity with horses and is so perceptive.
Her Majesty lets fate take its course—
and accepts what happens.
When it comes to horses, she always looks
forward and never dwells on the past.
She is never melancholy.
Instead, she is very level, accepting and
straightforward—I suppose that is what
has made her such an amazing monarch'

John Warren, The Queen's racing adviser, tells the *Daily Telegraph*
what was the secret of The Queen's success

Christmas Eve, which the young Princess aptly named Carol and Crackers.

The Queen's Pembroke Welsh corgis were all descended from Susan, an 18th-birthday present, and, from her accession, she owned 30 of them. Susan even accompanied her on her honeymoon. In 2012, three of them, Monty, Holly and Willow, trotted alongside James Bond as he escorted Her Majesty to a helicopter to make what appeared to be an unusual entry into the London Olympics.

'I doubt if I have ever encountered dogs who shared with their owners a quieter or serener companionship'

Our Princesses and Their Dogs (1936)

Towards the end of her life, The Queen made the decision not to breed any more dogs as she thought it unfair to leave a young one —Willow, the last of her full-breed corgis, died in April 2018. A few months before that, she had adopted a corgi named Whisper following the death of his owner, but he also died that October. She also had a number of 'dorgis', a cross-breed resulting from an unplanned liaison between a corgi ➤

Above. Corgis and dorgis tumble down the plane steps as they disembark ready for duty. *Facing page:* Private contentment

My family and other animals

It was not only dogs and horses that captured The Queen's interest

▶ The Queen was president of several pigeon-racing societies and used to regularly visit the royal loft at Sandringham (*left*), home to more than 200 birds. It was established in 1886, when Leopold II of the Belgians gave the Royal Family racing pigeons. One royal pigeon won a Dickin medal for its role in reporting a lost aircraft in the Second World War

▶ The Queen technically owned all mute swans in Britain and, in 2005, she claimed ownership of 88 cygnets on the Thames, which are looked after by the Swan Marker. The first royal Swan Keeper was appointed in about the 12th century

▶ Technically, The Queen also owned all the sturgeons (*below*), whales and dolphins in UK waters

▶ The Queen founded the Balmoral fold of Highland cattle (*right*) in 1953. The herd is now 100-head strong

▶ The Queen often received animals as gifts, including sloths from Brazil, black beavers from Canada, a canary from Germany, giant tortoises from the Seychelles (*left*) and an elephant called Jumbo from the Cameroon. All of the animals were given to London Zoo

and Princess Margaret's dachshund Pipkin. When at Buckingham Palace, the corgis and dorgis slept in raised wicker baskets in a special boot room near the royal apartments, where they wandered freely. When The Queen was being fitted for a dress, she carried a special magnet to pick up the pins to save the corgis pricking their paws.

The corgi is so synonymous with royalty that one forgets The Queen's equal devotion to gundogs. The kennels at Sandringham, established by Edward VII in 1879 to house 100 dogs, were home to gundogs, labradors and cocker spaniels of varying ages.

In the past, The Queen explained that she kept mainly labradors because she had felt it was the 'normal thing to do', following her father, George VI, who, in turn, continued the breeding programme of his father, George V, who founded the Sandringham strain of black labradors in 1911.

It seems, however, that the young Elizabeth wasn't content to just sit back and watch. At Balmoral, she would take the corgis onto the moor to help find the grouse. However, although the corgis were expert at locating the shot birds in the heather, they had difficulty retrieving them, so she would watch them wind the game and then rush over to retrieve the grouse herself.

'Her Majesty is a real countrywoman,' an approving Bill Meldrum, her former gundog trainer and former head keeper at Sandringham, told us in Diamond Jubilee year. From

'Had she not been who she was, she would like to be a lady living in the country with lots of horses and dogs'

Horace Smith, Princess Elizabeth's first riding instructor

1964, the two set out to bring new blood into the kennels and began a breeding programme. Her Majesty's ambition was to own a field-trial champion, a feat Mr Meldrum achieved five times over his 50-year tenure. Latterly, she had been breeding and working cocker spaniels, too, which she valued for their ability to retrieve game from difficult and dense cover.

The Queen's picking-up ability was well known. She would often collect four dogs (usually three labs and a cocker) from the kennels on the morning of a shoot day and, having loaded them into the back of her Range Rover, join the picking-up team. According to Mr Meldrum, she was 'a very good handler who has a great knowledge of what a dog should do'.

The late COUNTRY LIFE writer and countryman John Humphreys recalled a much-talked-about occasion that saw The Queen

A corgi joins the photograph of the World Cup-winning England rugby squad in 2008

make a memorable retrieve with her black labrador bitch Sherry. 'The story is told of a hard-hit grouse at Balmoral flying into the distance, but collapsing and dying on a tumulus of heather raised like a table above the surrounding moor.

'It was a long retrieve [about 800 yards] and, time and again, The Queen got the dog to the area, but, as it had flushed a live grouse from the same spot, she had difficulty persuading the dog to keep hunting on the peat hag. She was so involved she didn't realise the drive had ended and that the shooting party had gathered behind her.

'At last, Sherry hit the scent, picked the bird and came galloping back. There was a spatter of applause and The Queen was overcome with embarrassment, saying that she could never have done that had she known all those people were watching.'

Towards the end of her life, The Queen was not as involved with training, but she still worked her dogs at every opportunity and it was clear they were a great source of contentment. Some royal watchers suggested that Her Majesty's fondness for her dogs was because she didn't go to school as a child and so had few human playmates, but it seems to me that she was like anyone else who couldn't be without a labrador at their side —she simply adored her dogs. *PL*